T0334563

OFF THE MARK

OFF
THE MARK

How Grades, Ratings, & Rankings
Undermine Learning (but Don't Have To)

Jack Schneider and Ethan L. Hutt

Harvard University Press

Cambridge, Massachusetts | London, England

2023

Library of Congress Cataloging-in-Publication Data

Names: Schneider, Jack (Writer on education), author. | Hutt, Ethan L., author.
Title: Off the mark : how grades, ratings, and rankings undermine
learning (but don't have to) / Jack Schneider and Ethan L. Hutt.
Description: Cambridge, Massachusetts ; London, England : Harvard
University Press, 2023. | Includes bibliographical references and index.
Identifiers: LCCN 2022061113 | ISBN 9780674248410 (cloth)
Subjects: LCSH: Grading and marking (Students) | Grading and
marking (Students)—United States. | Education—Aims and objectives. |
Learning. | Educational accountability. | Education and state—United States.
Classification: LCC LB3051 .S3244 2023 | DDC 371.27/2—dc23/eng/20230113
LC record available at https://lccn.loc.gov/2022061113

For our students

Contents

OFF THE MARK

Introduction

We began work on this book before the COVID-19 outbreak swept across the globe. And as the pandemic shuttered schools, colleges, and universities, we wondered whether our project might suddenly be irrelevant amid such a massive disruption. In the early days, it seemed possible. Soon, however, we realized that grades, ratings, and rankings were more pertinent than ever.

With students learning from home, would their work be graded? Some young people had robust networks of support, while others were on their own; many lacked adequate internet connections. Given these disparities, could grading be done fairly? And would it actually measure learning? Or would it simply correlate with the extent to which students' lives had been turned upside down?

Assigning students grades wasn't the only evaluation practice disrupted by the pandemic. Each year, students across every level of schooling take millions of standardized tests. A cornerstone of nearly all these tests is that they are administered under the same conditions and, often, at exactly the same time. But the pandemic made assembling any number of students in one place for an hours-long examination not just unfeasible but unethical. Even so, the literal life and death stakes of the pandemic couldn't stop families and educators around the country from worrying about what the disruption in testing would mean for students. What would happen to young people enrolled in Advanced Placement courses? Could students take their exams from home? Would colleges still award them credit for their scores? What about students about to apply to college? Would the SAT and ACT tests still be given? Would colleges and universities still require them for admission? And what about state-mandated standardized tests? Would they be administered?

Those were just the questions of most immediate concern. Longer-term questions lingered, too: How would the disrupted learning of the pandemic school years be memorialized for future audiences on students' transcripts? Would courses that students could not complete still appear there? Should students' grades be accompanied by asterisks or perhaps converted to pass / fail? If schools adopted these policies, would students be given a choice about the form of their grade, or should schools unilaterally apply the new policies? Equity seemed to demand across-the-board solutions; but what about the students who had gone into the pandemic with A averages, which they had so assiduously maintained? Was it fair to wipe that away?

Faced with the possibility of their grades being converted to pass / fail, students at Harvard countered that any deviation in policy should stay in line with existing norms; instead of pass / fail, the students argued that Harvard should adopt a "double A" system that included two grades: an A and an A-minus.[1] This counterproposal only raised still more fundamental questions. Was a school's responsibility to protect the interests of its students? To ensure the general integrity of its grading system? To safeguard the fairness of the larger system of higher education?

The debates over these and related questions were fierce, and emotions ran hot. Parents started online petitions, advocacy groups filed lawsuits, and newspapers printed countless op-eds.[2] Even the *New York Times* ethicist felt compelled to weigh in on the equities at stake in these questions.[3] One thing was clear: problems with assessment definitely weren't going away.

Although it took a worldwide crisis to place these questions at the forefront of our discussion about education, the challenges they highlighted were with us all along. Consider some of the language we have for describing the problems and predicaments associated with educational assessment. How often have we heard complaints about teachers "teaching to the test" and students cramming for their exams, knowing full well that learning is beside the point? How often have students shrewdly identified the "gut" classes offering an "easy A," or fallen back on strategies like "grade grubbing" or "grade lawyering" for higher marks? Virtually everyone who has been to school is aware that any reference to one's "permanent record" is to be taken as a thinly veiled threat.

This enduring displeasure with what we call "assessment technologies"—the most notable of which are grades, tests, and transcripts—has fueled a cottage industry of critique. Scholars and self-proclaimed thought leaders have thoroughly documented shortcomings in the way schools measure and record student learning. Still more have offered prepackaged "solutions" to the problems associated with grading, rating, and ranking. Yet, despite more than a century of critique, they have by and large failed to alter the dominant approach to measuring student learning. Why is that?

The first reason is that our assessment practices are deeply intertwined with each other, with our educational institutions, and with other parts of society. This deep entanglement underlies virtually all of the questions raised by the pandemic. An altered grade or a missing test score during one year, families feared, would continue to reverberate well into the future. Likewise, the choices made by a single college or university could have rippling consequences across higher education and down through K–12 schools.

But there is another sense in which our assessment technologies are intertwined and, therefore, extremely resistant to change and prone to dysfunction. This is easily illustrated with an example that will be familiar to anyone who has issued or received a grade. Imagine that a teacher gives a student a C to communicate something along the lines of "Hey, this isn't your best work." The teacher knows that his pupil is bright and capable, and he wants to challenge her to rise to her potential. Yet the student receiving the C is mostly attuned to *anything but* what her teacher thinks he's saying. She knows that her parents will see that grade. And more importantly, she knows that college admissions officers and employers might someday look at her transcript; she's focused on keeping that permanent record blemish-free. Instead of hearing a gentle chiding, then, the student is likely hearing something more along the lines of "Watch out, because I can ruin your future." She might apply herself more diligently, but not in the way her teacher imagined, and not without some serious unintended consequences.

Despite these entangled purposes, policy leaders often approach reform in a piecemeal way, advocating for their preferred forms of assessment and decrying the rest. But this too often involves mistaking the tool for the task. We might not like the SAT or ACT as a feature of college admissions, for instance, but abolishing those tests won't eliminate the underlying issue that spurred and sustained their use for almost a century: the need to rate and rank students who have been exposed to different teachers, curricula, and school environments.

The challenge of comparison suggests the second reason why so little has changed despite so much displeasure: we *need* assessments. How else would we determine which students are placed in honors courses? What would be the process for handling students who move from one district to another, or from one state to another? How would colleges select qualified applicants for admission? How would employers sift through applications from inexperienced recent graduates? How would families know how their children are doing? How would taxpayers know how the local schools arc doing?

There are lots of ways of answering those questions. But many of us aren't prepared to do so without assessment results—particularly the practices of grading, rating, and ranking.

Part of the reason we need assessments is that they are a core element of the education system's infrastructure. It wasn't always this way. Over time, however, as academic success became important not only for further progress in school but also for job opportunities, we have asked our assessment technologies to take on more responsibilities for wider audiences. Today, they are incorporated into nearly every element of formal schooling, across both K–12 and higher education. Getting rid of them isn't as easy as replacing the computers in a media lab or the books in the library. It would require us to rethink almost every part of how we educate students.

But if the balance is so askew, and the complaints so perennial, why do we not demand radical change? Why is it that we wring our hands at the overreliance on grades and test scores, yet accept them as the primary evidence of what young people know and can do? How can we take seriously the fact that student transcripts summarize an entire academic career, despite rarely being longer than a Twitter post?

The answer to these questions is the third reason why we can't simply dump the practices of grading, rating, and ranking: we *believe* in them.

Whether we recognize it or not, we cast our votes in favor of grading, rating, and ranking nearly every day. We expect our children to be quizzed and tested, to receive grades for their performance, and to be sorted into class ranks. We expect them to sit for exams that purport to rate their aptitude and achievement. And we expect them to carry permanent records not only across their schooling experiences, but also into their professional lives. Sure, we worry about their stress levels, stay up late helping them, and lament their disappointments. We grouse and grumble about cramming and grade grubbing and the orientation toward tokens rather than learning. More often than not, though, we encourage them to play the game.

That's because a *real* school, we collectively believe, gives letter grades, preps students for high-stakes tests, and maintains permanent records. Sure, there are some exotic alternatives that embrace divergent assessment practices. But they're the exceptions that prove the rule. And even in those cases, when students get ready to apply for college, they generally need to sit for standardized examinations and produce transcripts with letter grades. Assessment, like death and taxes, is a misery to be endured.

Most of us believe this because we've never experienced anything different. Once upon a time, letter grades were introduced into our schools. Long ago, the first standardized test was given. And before any of us can remember, the transcript was born. Yet generations have passed since then. And because most adults spend more than a decade in the education system before sending their children to school, we develop particular views about what is normal. Expecting young people to have the same experience we did, we end up replicating the past even as we complain about the present.

Alternatives exist. In the United States and abroad, schools have developed different approaches to grading, rating, and ranking, many of which are familiar to us. Pass / fail grading, for instance, is something that many of us have experienced, as is the so-called narrative report card, which replaces or complements letter grades with a written account of student progress. But none of these, on its own, can hope to displace the existing approach to assessment that limits and constrains student learning. If any of these alternatives were sufficient, it would have changed the system by now.

So, what can be done? If past efforts have failed so badly, what chance do future efforts have at success?

This book is our attempt to respond to these questions. The answers we provide are informed by our research on the assessment of student learning. But they are also shaped by roughly two decades of work on the history and politics of school reform. This latter strand of scholarship, though less immediately relevant to the topic of the book, deeply informs our approach to the subject and our view of how educational change actually works. As a result, this book is built on three big ideas that shape our approach to this project, our analysis of the core issues, and our suggestions for reform.

First, as historians, we begin from the premise that the tools that we use to assess, record, and communicate about student learning were never obvious or preordained. Rather, we must understand them as the product of historical processes that reflect evolving beliefs and recurring conflicts about what schools should do, what students should learn, and what stakes should be attached to our desired outcomes. This historical approach is particularly useful for understanding how multiple layers of goals and functions have accumulated over time to produce our current practices. The implication of this observation is that if we want to understand our current set of practices, we need to start not with utopian ideas or high theory, but with a study of history.

Second, having studied decades of persistent failure in school reform, we also approach this project with a keen appreciation for how deeply intertwined the elements of our education system are with other aspects of the system, as well as with the competing politics and ideologies of the wider society. More often than not, reforms fail not because of bad ideas, but because of a failure to account for complexity and the unintended consequences of change. Policy leaders all too often believe they can change a single element in the system without particular attention to everything that element is entangled with. In this respect, it can be useful to think of the education system as we would an ecosystem. The flora and fauna within an ecosystem evolved under certain conditions and in specific relationship to each other. Efforts to introduce a new species are certain to reverberate in a host of expected and unexpected ways. Recognizing the complexity of a system doesn't mean that we shouldn't work to create change. It does, however, mean that we must take great care in understanding the *entire system*. As historians and scholars, we believe prior failures to reform our assessment technologies have been chiefly a product of simplistic thinking. A truckload of slogans and gimmicks has produced very little change. To do better, we must pay more attention to what lies beneath the surface, and we must seek solutions that respond to the complex environments in which they will be applied.

Third, and finally, schools are fundamentally conservative institutions. This observation is not a value judgment, but a fact. American reformers have never been short on radical ideas for reimaging schools; the reality, however, is that parents and teachers have been much less interested in trusting the well-being of young people to grand experiments. Change is hard because people prefer practices that, even when imperfect, have stood the test of time. And many of our assessment practices go back a long way. Our mentors, David Tyack and Larry Cuban, observed decades ago in their masterful treatise on school reform, *Tinkering Toward Utopia,* that teachers and administrators when faced with a reform effort tend to hybridize their practice—to take the best parts of the new and mix it with the old. This tendency to preserve existing practices and routines even as we work toward reform is part of the institutional conservatism of schools. We think reformers would be wise to remember this message about hybridization, which informs our thinking throughout the book.

These ideas lead us to take a measured view of the prospects for reform. That might disappoint some readers hoping to encounter a call for something more radical. But we don't think it forestalls meaningful change. Quite the opposite, actually. Recognizing the pragmatic conservatism of schools, we opt for a multipronged approach that invites concerned parents, educators, and leaders to consider their current practices, their degrees of freedom in crafting new policies, and the prevailing support for institutionalizing such work over time.

The first step to securing meaningful reform, and a central focus of our book, is to develop a clear sense of how our system operates. Such an understanding needs to be focused not just on naming problems, but also on describing the *how* and the *why* of our approach to assessing and recording student learning. To do so, we must start from the premise that, regardless of how we feel about them, our present technologies actually accomplish something important. As we discuss later in the book, there are three core functions of assessment:

- Motivation: to produce particular responses and elicit specific behaviors from students (e.g., compliance).
- Communication: to transmit "short-haul" messages (e.g., from teacher to parents) and "long-haul" messages (e.g., from school to future employer).
- Synchronization: to promote system-level coherence and operation (e.g., proving that a student has completed one "level" of schooling and is ready for the next).

To sustain learning in our schools, we can't just complain about grading, rating, and ranking. Instead, we need to replace those practices with something better. And, in so doing, we need to recognize that any new practices will need to continue performing existing functions. Thus, while we theoretically support a more radical move like abolishing grades, we pragmatically lean more toward a solution that would serve as a reasonable substitute. Our idea is to de-weaponize grades by making them "overwriteable"—that is, by embracing the idea that grades can and should be updated as students move toward mastery of a subject. It doesn't quite make for the same rallying cry as "No more grades!" (Imagine students chanting: "Go ahead and keep the grades but make them less high-stakes by allowing us to periodically alter them based on our improved skills!") But unlike the drive to abolish grading, it might actually be adopted during our lifetimes.

In short, we don't think that trying to assess student learning is the problem. Instead, we think the problem is that our present technologies are too clumsy for the work we want them to do. There are no silver bullets or panaceas. But there is much that we can accomplish if we are attuned to the core uses of grading, rating, and ranking, and to the root causes of our current problems with those practices.

Our astute readers will no doubt have noticed by this point that we have conspicuously avoided articulating a theory of learning. Where do we come down, a reader might wonder, on the question of how best to promote learning? After all, if we're making the claim that grades, ratings, and rankings have gotten in the way of learning, then we must have clear feelings about how students learn best.

We could try to answer that question. We've both studied with experts on the topic. We've worked closely with educators and school leaders. We have read broadly. Ultimately, however, this is not a book designed for people who subscribe to a single theory or approach. In our view, current assessment practices impede real learning regardless of what you think "real" learning looks like. Just as importantly, reformed assessment practices like those we describe later in the book are compatible with multiple theories of learning. We believe we can contribute most to this discussion not by weighing in on debates within the learning sciences, but by describing in detail the problems and challenges of grading, rating, and ranking. Our hope is that even if some readers disagree with our prescriptions for change, they will still find the book useful for driving forward their own vision of learning.

Even if readers accept all of these premises of the book, they still might wonder why they should spend time reading about a fairly niche topic like how we assess and record student learning. After all, the world is full of big problems that require our sustained attention. Even if we confine ourselves to the field of education, there are seemingly bigger problems than grades, tests, and transcripts. Segregation by race and class continue to worsen in the United States as our policymakers retreat from decades-old promises to make our schools inclusive. Inequitable funding ensures that the least advantaged all too often have the fewest resources. And in an increasing number of states, wide-reaching voucher programs now threaten the very premise of public education. Why, then, should we spend any time worrying about grades, ratings, and rankings?

The answer is that learning matters.

We believe in the core principles of public education—that it should be democratically controlled, free of charge, and open to all. We also believe that our schools can and should be engines of racial and economic justice. But our schools must have learning at the center, especially if we wish for them to advance the aim of equity. And we have serious concerns about the extent to which that can happen under the existing assessment regime. Grading, rating, and ranking distort learning in fundamental ways, beginning in early elementary school and carrying across secondary and postsecondary education. It's only because they do so in such a complete and thorough manner that most of us have become accustomed to it.

Yet we can be shaken from our complacency. All it takes is a clearer picture of what an alternative might look like.

So, what's the last citadel of learning in our system? Where is the *process* of education still at the center? Many elite private schools have worked hard to cultivate this image of themselves. But one needn't fork over five-figure tuition in order to see a classroom centered around inquiry, play, discovery, and joy. Such classrooms are located in every community across the United States and around the world: they're called kindergartens.

As we were working on this project, we dropped in on a local school to watch five- and six-year-olds classifying insects. The classrooms bustled with activity—young people were immersed in animated conversations, drawing pictures, explaining their work to their teachers, and cheerfully engaging with their two guests. As students scurried about, we asked their teachers how they would evaluate student work on the project, and their answers surprised us. We knew that students wouldn't earn letter grades for the work or sit for an end-of-course standardized test. We knew they wouldn't have permanent records or class ranks. But what we hadn't anticipated was just how detailed and thoughtful the teachers' evaluation plans were. Of course, they were assessing student progress and offering feedback to their pupils; it shouldn't have surprised us at all. They just weren't using the technologies that have so thoroughly infiltrated higher levels of the system.

Focused on student learning, rather than on the demands of assessment technologies, Ms. Kennedy and Ms. Porter had created vibrant and engaging classrooms. Their students wanted to be there—in fact, at the end of the day, a few of them refused to leave, so busy were they on their insect projects. We left the school brimming with hope about what can happen in school.

We then drove down the road to the local high school and talked with teachers there. "What would it look like if the school got rid of grades, tests, and transcripts?" we asked. And almost all of the teachers we talked to responded in the same way: by laughing at us. "They wouldn't do the work," one of them said. "Parents would freak out," another told us. "Students want their grades," a third teacher responded. "They want good grades, good scores, perfect records—that way they can get into a good college."

Students in the early grades aren't learning calculus or writing essays, it's true. But the academic work they are doing is every bit as ambitious and rich in rigor as it is in later grade levels. Young students are developing the ability to read and write, to reason mathematically, and to explain the world as scientists do. And yet there is a major difference: their intellectual work is often guided by the inherent value of learning—the drive to understand, the thrill of knowing, and the delight of getting better at something that feels like it matters. We found ourselves wishing that could be true at every grade level and in every classroom, all the way through college and graduate school.

Now, it is important to note that kindergarten isn't always a refuge from the influence of grading, rating, and ranking. As recent research has found, accountability pressures have in many cases "trickled down" into the early grades. And the ultimate impact on teaching and learning, as one group of scholars found, is that many kindergarten teachers are devoting "more time to advanced literacy and math content, teacher-directed instruction, and assessment," while spending "substantially less time on art, music, science, and child-selected activities."[4] But we still see a different approach to learning that inspires us, and that makes us wish that subsequent levels of schooling were similarly full of joy and meaning.

We aren't suggesting that we have a simple fix, or that all of the world's classrooms should look like the kindergarten classrooms we visited. That would be a much shorter book, featuring much younger students. Instead, this book sets the stage for a more complex set of policy proposals that *might actually work*—an approach that might restore the balance required for real learning to occur in our elementary, secondary, and higher education systems. Building on a decade of research, this book explores the past, present, and future of how we measure student learning. Directed at a wide range of readers—including parents, teachers, and school administrators—it offers a starting point for conversations about how and why we evaluate students, as well as for how we might do it better. Though the book looks particularly at the United States, it is not a narrow domestic treatise. Instead, it tells a surprisingly global story. As Chapter 6 makes clear, grading, rating, and ranking in the United States is not markedly different from what happens in the rest of the world. Details may change—A–F grading, for instance, might be A–E grading in other countries, or 1–10 grading, or 1–20—but the broad contours of the story are mostly the same.

Because we anticipate a set of readers with potentially distinct interests in our subject matter, we offer a quick word about the organization of the book to help readers engage with it most effectively. The book is organized into three parts that explore, in turn, the present, past, and future of assessment. In Part I, we begin with a look at our three chief technologies for assessing student learning: grades (Chapter 1), tests (Chapter 2), and transcripts (Chapter 3). We suspect that many pieces of the arguments we develop in these first three chapters will be familiar to our readers—that our current grading systems, for instance, incentivize students to go through the motions rather than commit to learning—but we try to locate these complaints in the overall organization and structure of our education system. In describing and diagnosing our current practices and their many faults, we develop a foundation for thinking about what issues we need to address and why.

Having developed this assessment in Part I, you might suspect that Part II would be about solutions—how to fix the problems we've identified. But that would leave us without a crucially important perspective critical to getting it right in the future: a clear view of the past. In Part II, then, we set out to answer the question we hear so frequently from exasperated parents: How did it get like this? Believe it or not, there was a time before grades and standardized examinations existed—a time when no records of student achievement were ever committed to paper. As we explore in Chapter 4, these practices developed over time and in response to very particular challenges, and in Chapter 5 we trace how these developments coalesced into our current culture of assessment. Recapturing this past reminds us that there was nothing natural or inevitable about our current practices.

With past and present firmly in view, we can think about what assessment might look like in the future, if stakeholders are committed to change. Part III of the book opens with a look at the rest of the world. In Chapter 6, we examine the ways in which other countries face similar challenges. In Chapter 7, we turn back to the United States, looking at experimentation large and small. Finally, in Chapter 8, we consider how the insights provided by the two prior chapters point the way forward to a future in which we do more to sustain learning inside our schools, colleges, and universities.

We believe our suggestions reflect both the wisdom and humility that a clear understanding of our current system can impart. But we also hope that the arguments and ideas in this book will become the basis for concerned parents, educators, and system leaders to begin conversations in their own communities about the current state of assessment. It's long past time to tilt the balance back toward what matters most: learning.

PART I

Grading, Rating, Ranking

Undermining Learning

1

How Grades Fail

*T*he most obvious problem with grading is the fact that it's so effective at motivating students.

That may seem counterintuitive. How can success be a problem? Yet consider what, precisely, students are motivated to do when they strive for an A. It often doesn't have much to do with learning.

Grades function as a kind of crutch in K-12 and higher education. Rather than instilling an intrinsic love of learning in students, our system for the most part motivates them *extrinsically*—with grades.[1] As a result, students may learn something as they progress from kindergarten through higher education, but often only incidentally, in the pursuit of the rewards they're actually after. This isn't to say that students don't develop academic skills or that they never develop a real passion for the things they study. But as any teacher who has been asked "Is this going to be on the test?" can tell you, students' decisions about how they approach their schoolwork are strongly influenced by strategic considerations around grading.

In the eyes of students, education often has value only because it can be traded for something else—namely, social and economic advantage. The badges and honors of school, students have been taught, will gain them access to good colleges, good jobs, and good lives. As a result, grades have become like scrip money or Disney Dollars. They may not be legal tender, but they are certainly tokens of exchange, securing access to everything from gifted and talented programs to car insurance discounts.

This may seem harmless enough. But the emphasis on grades, rather than on learning, undermines the inherent value of education. We may tell young people that we want them to develop a love of learning, and that school is a place where they can discover, develop, and realize their potential. Yet what we incentivize them to do is usually quite different. When students stay up late cramming for an exam, when they copy their friends' homework, and when they pester their teachers for higher marks, they are showing us the messages they've received.

To be clear, getting good grades doesn't preclude students from developing a deep love of learning. Moreover, straight-A students may learn some important skills and develop productive habits as they scramble to compile their perfect report cards. But the crucial point is that our system is set up in such a manner that learning may be incidental to most of what happens as young people progress through the education system. Here, one of our mentors, David Labaree, is worth quoting at length:

> Students at all levels quickly come to the conclusion that what matters most is not the knowledge they learn in school but the credentials they acquire there. Grades, credits, and degrees—these become the objects to be pursued. The end result is to reify the formal markers of education and displace the substantive content. Students

learn to do what it takes to acquire the necessary credentials, a process that may involve learning some of the subject matter (at least whatever is likely to be on the next test) but also may not . . . The payoff for a particular credential is the same no matter how it was acquired, so it is rational behavior to try to strike a good bargain, to work at gaining a diploma, like a car, at a substantial discount.[2]

The reality of this situation is so deeply ingrained that even the smallest deviation under the most extraordinary circumstances produces backlash. Consider, for instance, the expression of dismay from Oregon parents when that state's department of education decided to suspend grading during the initial coronavirus outbreak of 2020. Many parents, no doubt, took the policy in stride. But signatories to an online petition were irate. Some wanted to know how to motivate their children without the brass ring of grades. As one mother complained: "How do I explain to my child that has great grades that she should keep working hard when anything that is D- and above will still 'pass'? This is ridiculous."[3]

Other parents were more concerned about the grades themselves. In short, they wanted their children to receive the tokens they were owed. As one parent commented on the petition: "GPA matters, let students earn their grades and be rewarded." And as another parent noted: "My HS student has worked his butt off for his grades and the wind was sucked right out of his sail."[4]

The upshot of this system is that for many students, school is simply the context in which they work to collect grades. In that sense, they aren't really students at all—they're employees. Their job descriptions are written on course syllabi and determined by the assignments that will be graded. Their pay, in turn, comes not in the form of a weekly paycheck, but in the form of quarterly grades. One student, making the case for assessment in the wake of the coronavirus pandemic, argued that letter grades provide "compensation."[5] And as one parent noted: "My daughter deserves the opportunity to receive grades to remain competitive with other HS students in other states and receive the appropriate accreditation for her hard work."[6]

In sum, grades motivate students, but they don't always motivate learning.

Rational Students, Irrational Outcomes

In pointing out that students are motivated to earn good grades irrespective of what they learn, we want to be clear that we are not blaming students or their parents for this behavior. Collectively, in the United States and around the globe, we have accepted a system that strongly incentivizes students to act strategically—to hustle their way to good grades by working smarter, rather than harder. While some might argue that this is itself a useful life skill, we think most people would agree that such an outcome is not what school is all about.[7]

Consider the phenomenon of grade grubbing—the practice of pestering instructors for higher marks, particularly on high-stakes assessments. Writing on the website of the academic journal *Science,* Adam Ruben reflected on his own experience as a grade-obsessed student: "The grade was everything. The grade was the all-important, all-consuming, all-powerful proxy for my identity as a student. I wasn't about to let it slip through my fingers when I had a possible shot at a higher one." What did he do, then, when he received a grade lower than what he aspired to? He confronted the instructor and "argued the hell out of that one point."[8]

From his perspective as an instructor, Ruben observed that his own students were no different than he was at their age. They begged, bargained with, and berated their instructor in pursuit of better grades—not "because they like points," but rather, "because the education system has told them that these points are the currency with which they can buy a successful future."[9] Ruben was stunned by the fact that his students were simply responding as rational actors, operating intelligently within a system that rewards this kind of behavior.

Grade grubbing of the kind that Ruben describes may be relatively rare. Many students are likely to simply accept the grades they're given, even if they're dissatisfied. But the fact that grade grubbing happens at all is evidence of the value that young people place on grades as the ultimate end product of education.

Cheating is the most extreme manifestation of this attitude. Whatever it may indicate about students, it also shows us something powerful about the incentives created by grades. Consider, for instance, a study that sought to understand whether and why college students decided to cheat. As the authors of the study concluded, "The most important reason why the students in our sample cheated was the 'desire to get ahead.'" To the surprise of the research team, that motivation was more important than variables like "attitude towards cheating," "opportunity to cheat," "cultural or moral acceptance of cheating as an established norm," "low risk of detection," or "heavy time demands."[10]

As instructors at all levels know, it isn't just college students who are motivated to cheat. As another researcher studying the motivations of cheating put it, the problem of cheating "starts early and increases as students move through school." As he found, grades played a central role: "Many students told me they know cheating is wrong, and they are not proud of their behavior. However, they feel they have to cheat to get the grades they need."[11]

Who cheats? Such questions are difficult to answer, given the powerful incentive for students to keep that information to themselves. Nevertheless, it seems that a majority of students find themselves operating outside of the rules at some point. According to one survey, 64 percent of students reported that they had cheated on a test.[12] And as one researcher found, parents were often complicit, doing "most of the work" on important take-home assignments.[13]

Even the most morally upright students are often looking for the quickest way to earn the most points. For evidence, look no further than the persistent inquiry from students about whether a particular topic will be on a subsequent test. What they are saying, in essence, is that if they know what they'll be tested on, they can avoid wasting their time studying things that won't "count." It's a classic shortcut that allows students to focus on what really matters: their grades.

Unequal Exchange

Schools are widely perceived as meritocratic institutions. That is, they are presumed to reward talent and hard work rather than inherited advantage. Yet the highest grades are all too often the reserve of a privileged minority of students. Why is that?

One factor is parents. Aware of the uses to which grades can be put, middle- and upper-class parents are a backstop against bad grades, and, as noted in the study above, a quiet driver of grade inflation. As David Labaree writes, "It is elite parents that see the most to gain from the special distinctions offered by a stratified education system, and therefore they are the ones who play the game of academic one-upmanship most aggressively."[14] Those least in need of academic support, in other words, are the most likely to be the squeaky wheels. Privileged parents will urge their children to reach out to teachers for help, will connect their children with tutoring, and will themselves intervene to ensure that grades never slip below the B-range.

The greatest inequities, however, may be a product of unconscious influence. As indicated by a large body of educational research, the strongest predictors of student achievement are family and neighborhood context. Teachers, of course, matter; but not as much as the out-of-school environment. To some extent, this is a direct function of resource inequality—of the difference between what can be purchased by higher-income earners and lower-income earners. But it seems that parental expectations matter more than family resources. That doesn't mean that affluent parents are better at raising children. Instead, they are more likely to exert pressure on students—in forms both subtle and overt—to succeed in school and bring home high marks. As research indicates, they do things like make regular inquiries about their children's marks, and are likely to discuss the importance of grades for all manner of life outcomes.[15]

While grades can motivate some students to work harder in school, at least at particular kinds of tasks, they can also have a demotivating effect. Students with 4.0 grade point averages (GPAs) have a lot to lose. By contrast, their lower-scoring peers—students who are often already systematically underserved—often see little to gain by exerting additional effort. If you're a C or D student, working harder seems like a bad bet. If learning is presented as work, and grades are presented as pay, why would you labor for a reward that never arrives?

Students from all backgrounds can be demotivated by grades. But once more, it tends to play out in ways that exacerbate inequities. Young people from low-income families and historically marginalized racial groups are more likely to start school behind their more privileged peers. And, as research demonstrates, they are likely to stay behind.[16] This is a complicated matter, associated with a number of variables. But key among them is what researchers refer to as "academic self-concept." As one set of scholars notes: "academic self-concept refers to individuals' knowledge and perceptions about themselves in achievement situations."[17] In other words, it describes the extent to which students view themselves as academically capable. Young people who start behind are likely to view themselves as less capable. And schools are often designed around competitive or individual processes that reinforce such perceptions and stereotypes about who succeeds in school. Even those students who do succeed are burdened with the responsibility of navigating multiple cultural codes among peer, community, and school environments.[18]

Many educators recognize this problem. In fact, there are school models that seek to disrupt and reshape students' academic self-concept. The Comer School Development Program, for instance, is rooted in the idea that schools must first help children develop "positive emotional bonds with school staff" and "a positive attitude toward the school program." Only then, the model suggests, can learning occur.[19] But this is hardly typical. More often, existing systems send the message to students that they don't have what it takes. Bad grades make official what many students already feel about themselves: that they are not good at academic work. This isn't to say that student self-esteem should come before academic challenge. But academic challenge can be encouraged without grading, ranking, and rating students.

Of course, even the best students at the most elite schools are not well served by this state of affairs. Talk to these students about their schoolwork and you're likely to get an earful about the strategic considerations surrounding their choices of Advanced Placement (AP) courses and the general state of competition for grades in their schools. Even schools that have tried to lower the temperature on the competition among students—for instance, by capping the number of AP courses each student can take in a year, which also places a cap on the highest possible GPA. But that does not eliminate the competition; it only restricts the playing field.

The Rate of Inflation

Students aren't the only ones to alter their behavior in response to grades. For at least two generations, observers have been wringing their hands over the scourge of "grade inflation." Teachers, they argue, are watering down standards in an effort to make everyone happy. The result, according to one scholar, is that teachers are depriving students "of appropriate academic challenges or an accurate picture of their knowledge, skills, and abilities."[20]

Yet instructors aren't simply being nice. Another way to understand grade inflation is as teachers' reasonable responses to the increasing "weaponization" of grades. Aware of the tremendous weight that grades can play in students' academic careers and their lives beyond school, instructors are often wary of issuing grades that will permanently label students and haunt them via their transcripts for years to come. The more enduring and summative a grade is—that is, the more it functions as a final evaluation of what a student knows and can do in a subject—the higher the stakes are. Will a D-plus on a three-question reading quiz alter a student's life? Almost certainly not. But a single D-plus on a student's high school transcript might be the difference between attending a dream college or a safety school.

The more that hangs in the balance for students, the harder it can be for instructors to "hold the line" and ignore the larger ramifications of their grading decisions. Consider the college professor who teaches an introductory course at an institution with a large percentage of first-generation students eligible for federal grant aid. The professor knows that such students often struggle academically in the first year as they make the transition from high school to college-level work. She also knows that in order to maintain eligibility for their Pell Grants, the students need to maintain a grade point average of 2.0—the equivalent of a C. Is the professor being unreasonable in thinking that grades in her first-year course ought not jeopardize students' ability to continue their college educations? A similar conundrum, if not outright moral dilemma, hung over nearly all grading decisions during the Vietnam War, when instructors knew that a student who flunked out would lose his draft deferment. Not surprisingly, colleges around the country saw a very steep rise in student GPAs during the period.[21]

Though not wanting students to be drafted into an unpopular war might be an extreme example, it nevertheless underscores the extent to which large and small dilemmas like these—where course grades become bound up in much larger, more consequential societal systems—suffuse our education system. Bad grades can keep students out of advanced coursework, can block them from participating in sports, and can even prevent them from graduating. Beyond that, grades play a role in university and graduate school admissions, and they play an important role in the initial screening for many employers, including the military.

Consequently, teachers and professors are leery of giving bad grades. There has been a steady upward shift in grading—a phenomenon that has played out in both K-12 and higher education. According to one analysis of college and university grading, 43 percent of all grades at American four-year institutions have been either an A or an A-minus. At some elite schools like Harvard, the median grade is now an A-minus, which puts it only slightly higher than the average for all private institutions, which see just under half (48 percent) of their students earning As.[22]

Researchers have found a similar upward trend in high school grades. According to a comprehensive study of grades in North Carolina between 2005 and 2016, the median high school GPA rose consistently throughout the decade. Though both affluent and less affluent high schools saw an increase in GPAs during this period, affluent high schools saw their GPAs rise at a faster rate. While less affluent high schools saw student GPAs increase by 0.17 (on a 4.0 scale), more affluent high schools saw an increase of 0.27.[23]

Some schools have responded to grade inflation by trying to place student grades in a larger context. For instance, many high schools provide information about class rank—a way to place a student's GPA in context. Similar efforts have been undertaken to varying degrees at the college level. A proposal by the Cornell University Faculty Senate in the 1990s, for instance, sought to publish the median grades for all courses, as well as to include the median course grade on student transcripts—allowing any reader of the transcript to understand the overall grading difficulty of the course. The policy, however, was only partially implemented: the course information was published on the internet for those willing to search for it, but it never appeared on transcripts. The result? Students used the newly available information to seek out more leniently graded courses, and soon the median GPA was once more on the rise. Ironically, a policy aimed at suppressing grade inflation managed to fuel it instead.[24]

Unfortunately, teachers' efforts to disarm grades by compressing the grading scale is only partially successful, because the shift in grades does not address the underlying competition in the system, which makes small distinctions among students highly consequential. As a result, the cycles of grade inflation become self-perpetuating: each uptick in the average grade places more pressure on both students and instructors to respond in kind. If one's peers are strategically selecting courses to maximize their GPAs and their relative class rankings, a student is forced at least to consider the wisdom of doing the same herself, lest she compare unfavorably when competing for graduate school or a sought-after job. Educators, likewise, find themselves pressured to make do with an increasingly narrow band of the grading scale. Few reputations precede an educator quite like one's reputation as a tough grader. College and university instructors, particularly those early in their careers, are especially sensitive to being seen as engaged in a rearguard action against grade inflation, especially given the evidence that student grades correlate with student course evaluations. The higher the grades, the higher the course gets rated.

With the incentives aligned the way they are, it is easy both to explain grade inflation and to see why it continues. The few pockets of resistance to grade inflation—an economics department here, an "old school" English teacher there—are little match for the systematic forces that perpetuate these trends.

Decoding the Mixed Messages: Short-Haul and Long-Haul Communication

Having laid out some of the key uses of grades in schools, we can begin to see the problem: we want grades to do too many things. We want grades to motivate, to communicate to audiences near and far, and to record these messages succinctly for posterity. It is no wonder that we find that grades are not always up to the task. As we think about how we might better understand and improve this situation, it is useful to disentangle these purposes and to develop some language to speak more precisely about these differing functions.

In particular, it is useful to distinguish between two kinds of communication conveyed by grades: "short-haul" communication and "long-haul" communication. Short-haul communication is the communication that grades facilitate between the teacher and the student or between the school and the family. It is this short-haul function of grades that is envisioned by school policies requiring teachers to issue "progress reports" or that require parents to sign or acknowledge the receipt of a student's report card. The whole idea is that parents and students receive these communications in a timely way and can respond to the information—by making a plan to work a bit harder, by getting some extra help, or by establishing clearer parental oversight. At the end of the year, such communications can also be the basis for conversations among families, teachers, and counselors about next year's course schedule.

In contrast to short-haul communications, which generally occur within the several blocks or several miles that most students live from their schools, long-haul communication travels much farther. Carrying information via the official transcript (the subject of

Chapter 3), grades end up communicating with unknown audiences—college admissions boards, scholarship committees, employers—at great remove from the specific school or community in which the grades were originally issued.

One characteristic of long-haul communication is that the immediate context in which the grade was received is no longer readily evident. Yes, some schools try to include some contextual information in these long-haul messages; but these small bits of information—class rank, average GPA, instructor name—only underscore the extent to which substantive context has been stripped away. While counselors, teachers, and families are often well aware of all the academic and nonacademic influences on students' grades, the grades on the transcript appear pristine on the page. This is obviously a major reason why students engage in strategic behavior around grading. If students, often with the help of their parents, can get the "right" teachers, or at least avoid the notoriously hard graders, they can reduce the risk that bad grades pose to their futures. Likewise, the student who coaxed a higher grade from her teacher ultimately has a transcript indistinguishable from the student who earned the grade outright.

There is a long running debate among admissions officers and scholars about the value of students' GPAs in the college and university admissions process. On the one hand, some argue that GPAs embody the collective judgments of multiple educators across multiple years. On the other hand, some argue, GPAs represent a muddled signal full of subjective teacher judgments about effort, improvement, and, worst of all, local norms around grade inflation. These critics argue that this is why the information provided by standardized tests like the SAT or the ACT is a necessary addition to student applications. Advocates on both sides of this debate can point to rigorous evidence supporting the competing propositions that GPAs are a better predictor of student success than SAT scores, or that SAT scores provide additional, independent information about the likelihood of success not captured by GPAs. Wherever one stands on this debate, though, what should not be lost is that both sides are expecting a new and different use of grades: they are thinking about grades not as an indication of *past* performance (though they are that), but rather, about their value in predicting *future* performance.

Employers are another audience for the long-haul communication provided by grades. Over time, we have seen a steady increase in both the formal and informal education requirements for jobs ranging from lawyer to barber. Indeed, there is considerable evidence that employers have strong preferences for people with good grades and credentials even when they have no direct bearing on the job requirements. These preferences tend to rise and fall with the overall state of the labor market: when the market for employment is tight, such requirements fall away; when there are lots of people looking for work, employers rediscover their preference for credentials.[25]

Human capital theorists, and economists more generally, have their own explanation for this. Grades, they argue, provide a useful signal about a person's skill set. The same is true about credentials and degrees, which at their most basic level represent a bundle of at least passing grades. Depending on the instance, a credential may be enough of a message about one's qualifications for a job. In other cases, an employer might want to know not just whether someone passed her classes, but whether the grades on her transcript indicate that she excelled and ranked at the top of her class. To be sure, even with this additional information, the signal offered by grades is a noisy one. But when we consider the alternatives, relying strictly on personal referrals, fleeting impressions, or, worst of all, stereotypes, the use of grades makes sense. Indeed, there is evidence that if employers rely on signals like grades or credentials, they will be less likely to rely on gendered and racialized stereotypes about workers' potential productivity.[26] Nevertheless, it remains true that grades tell employers very little about what an individual knows and can do relative to a particular set of work tasks. This makes students' obsession with maximizing grades both more legitimate—employers *do* consider them signals—and also more absurd, as the underlying substance that the grade represents is hardly relevant except in the broadest possible sense.

Miscommunication and Garbled Messages

These multiple messages, conveyed to audiences near and far, are what place teachers and students in such a difficult position. A report card full of grades once carried home on a piece of paper to be read, discussed, and discarded now have an uncomfortable permanence—a record that can be difficult to outrun. No wonder instructors have used a smaller and smaller range of grades over time. For some students today, a B-plus is a disaster. What, then, is an educator to do?

One response by teachers has been to use written feedback to communicate with students. If grades can no longer really function as communication devices, then perhaps actual words can. The challenge, however, is one of scale. Most teachers at public high schools, for instance, teach five sections of roughly twenty students each—one hundred or more students a day. If teachers spend just over a minute reading and commenting on each student assignment, grading will take two hours. If they dedicate more time to the effort—spending ten minutes per student reading an essay, for instance—it can take an entire weekend.

The result can be burnout. Certainly not all teachers face such intimidating grading burdens. But for those who do, it can be the worst part of the job. As one teacher wrote online: "I love teaching. Grading? Not so much. There have been plenty of times when my family has found me pounding my head on my desk, asking why I assigned so many written assessments. (The bottom line is that they help my students grow and become fully ready for college or career, but I digress.) . . . I'm estimating that teachers spend between five to 10 hours a week on grading."[27]

Perhaps the biggest problem is that students often don't *read* this feedback. Because the grades are what really matter, students often flip to the back of their papers—right past any commentary offered by teachers—to see their marks. Once the prize has been fetched from the bottom of the metaphorical cereal box, papers often end up stuffed in the bottom of backpacks or tossed in waste baskets. As one writing instructor reflected: "As a high school English teacher, and later as a teaching assistant for a writing-across-the-curriculum program, I often was frustrated by having to repeat the same comments to many students, and I resented the time spent writing the same comments on students' second and third papers as on their first."[28]

Research has found that students infrequently act on instructor feedback.[29] And why would they? Once the grade has been recorded, students turn their gaze to the next task. This is not to say that clever educators haven't devised ways to try to coax their students into attending to feedback—requiring students to submit multiple versions of their work, for instance, or incorporating a reflective component after assignments are returned—or that some students aren't intrinsically motivated to strive for personal growth and improvement. But to the extent that educators do this as a countermeasure, we must concede that we have built a system in which our assessment technologies are dictating pedagogy and not vice versa.

Surprising Benefits and Disturbing Distortions

If our goal is to create a better system, we need to be as clear about the virtues of our grading system as we are about its faults. Though grades have many drawbacks, and despite the fact that they often reward strategic gaming rather than deep learning, we need to point out that there are some upsides as well.

While many people critique grades for being too subjective, our willingness to accept grades at face value should be acknowledged as one of the core strengths of our system. The willingness of educators and schools to honor the professional judgments of fellow educators—expressed in the form of grades—is a key part of why grades serve as an effective currency. Imagine what would happen if the University of California system, citing the considerable achievement and resource disparities among high schools in the state, decided that students who receive grades lower than a B-minus, and who attend lower-achieving high schools, would no longer be considered as having passed those classes.

If this strikes you as grossly unfair, it's because you have some sense of the necessity for establishing the formal equity of grades—that is, declaring by rule that all identical grades will be treated the same way within the school system.[30] In this case, we give credence to and leverage the decontextualized character of grades. We may know in reality that not all As are the same, but the fact that we officially treat them as if they *are* the same lends a modicum of fairness to the system.

This isn't a mere hypothetical. Establishing the equity of grades at the system level and fostering the mutual recognition of these judgments is actually the basis for a number of laws intended to counteract the inequities in our system. States like California and Texas, for instance, have developed "percent plans" for admission into their state university systems. A student who graduates in the top 10 percent of her class in a Texas high school is automatically granted admission to a University of Texas campus of her choosing. This is not because people think that an A at one school represents the exact same amount of learning as an A at another school. Instead, it is a recognition that the grade should stand within the context it was given and not be subjected to additional questioning. The same basic approach is enshrined in virtually all community college systems, where admission is offered on the basis of securing passing grades in prior coursework rather than on an additional external benchmark. Though many colleges and universities still rely on placement examinations to adjust for differences in students' academic preparation, the fact that this assessment happens *after* enrollment only underscores the extent to which the equality of grades and schools is honored throughout the system. A student who needs remediation in a specific subject in order to advance further is not prevented from being recognized as a high school graduate or a college student.

This kind of formalized equity in grading preserves a degree of lateral and upward mobility in a system rife with inequality. These practices are also key parts of our education system and help prevent the system from falling further out of balance. We highlight them because, as we consider alternatives to our current practices, we need to make sure we do not undermine supportive features of the current system.

Making the Grade

Grades are a distortive force in American schools. Whatever their benefits, and there *are* benefits, it is hard to escape the fundamental truth that grades only periodically motivate deep learning. More frequently, they encourage students to go through a series of motions: turning in daily assignments, preparing for exams, participating in class, and producing assessments that align with expectations. As we have experienced ourselves as students and educators, learning can and often does occur along the way. Much of the time, however, learning is beside the point, at least in the minds of students. Young people, smart as they are, learn quickly that a grade is valuable not for the learning that it reflects, but for its future exchange-value—that it can be traded in for parental praise, college admission, or a good job. This kind of commodification is directly in tension with the goal of many educators and the hopes of many citizens, that schools will foster an intrinsic love of learning in students.

As we have tried to highlight, a key source of this distortion—the emphasis on grade attainment rather than on learning—is the result of the short- and long-haul messages we have asked grades to carry in our system. We want them to communicate intimately with parents and students, offering them a heads-up or a nudge on the need to improve. But at the same time, we want them to communicate in a formal way with audiences that are years in the future. In this mode, they must offer an official judgment about how students rank among their peers, about their knowledge and skills, and, by extension, about their likelihood of success at future endeavors. It is no wonder, then, that teachers and students feel that grades occupy such a prominent place in schooling. As much as we might like to believe that grades are just conversations about work done in the classroom, it's always clear that something bigger is at stake.

2

This Is a Test

*I*n a classroom set-
ting, test scores are
frequently used by teachers to inform A–F grades. The scores from
those kinds of assessments—an end-of-unit chemistry test, for
instance—are really just a part of the grading system that shapes
teaching and learning.

Standardized tests, however, are different.

Unlike their classroom counterparts, standardized assessments
operate independently from the school curriculum. Moreover, the
results of standardized testing—like Advanced Placement (AP) exam
scores, or SAT scores—live on students' records and follow them
into the future (a subject we discuss more in Chapter 3). Because
standardized test scores provide such unique, comparative pieces of
information, and often at key moments in the school process, students and families have little choice but to take these tests and their
results seriously.

Most discussion about standardized testing and its consequences concerns the rating and ranking of schools. Since the very

first standardized tests were given in American public schools in the nineteenth century, the scores they produce have made headlines and been a source of concern for the public. In both the past and the present, schools have responded in a variety of predictable ways to raise their scores. This has been especially true since 2002, when the federal government's No Child Left Behind (NCLB) law instituted a slate of penalties for low test score performance. Consequences like teaching to the test, narrowing of the curriculum, and cheating are all well-documented results of high-stakes testing.

Our concern is somewhat different. Though we do explore the impact of state-run standardized testing in this chapter, we are chiefly concerned with the way that test scores are used to rate and rank individual students.

As with grades, standardized tests can distort student learning and restrict opportunity. Too often, though, opponents of standardized tests fail to distinguish among them and instead opt for blanket assertions about the harmful effects of standardized testing, leading to confused or muddled calls for their elimination or replacement. Before we get to questions of reform, we need more clarity about the multiple and enduring uses of standardized tests in our system. Understanding how these purposes contribute to and sustain our love-hate relationship with tests, despite centuries of well-worn critiques, is crucial for seeing the possibilities for change.

Places, Everyone

Students enter school with vastly different levels of academic preparation, and with highly disparate needs. In response, those in the early grades are regularly given assessments like the Dynamic Indicators of Basic Early Literacy Skills (DIBELS) or the Measures of

Academic Progress (MAP). These tests are diagnostic in nature—they are designed to assess what students know and what their academic strengths and weaknesses are.

There are many different kinds of diagnostic tests. Some, called norm referenced tests, are intended to help place students within a particular distribution (e.g., "Sally is in the 85th percentile of 8-year-old readers"). These tests are often given for the purpose of identifying students who are particularly advanced or who need extra assistance. Other diagnostic tests, called criterion referenced tests, are intended to assess whether a student has reached a particular learning standard (e.g., "Bobby is at grade-level in letter identification."). As standards in American education have become more explicit and more detailed in the last few decades, these kinds of diagnostic tests have become more common in American classrooms. In whatever combination diagnostic tests are used, the likelihood is that by the time students have made it through several years of schooling, their schools and their teachers will have a statistical portrait of them drawn by these scores.

The information from these tests, once it is recorded in a school's files, will almost certainly shape a student's trajectory through the education system. Like standardized tests themselves, this is not necessarily a bad thing. Early diagnostic tests can be critical in identifying a student as eligible for extra services—assistance with English language acquisition, for instance, or help overcoming a learning disability—and are key to intervening before an initial difference becomes a persistent disadvantage. Research shows that at every level of schooling, from kindergarten through higher education, identifying weaknesses and providing targeted support can make a huge difference in school outcomes. There is no question that in many contexts these tests and the information they provide to educators are crucial tools in securing educational equity.

If diagnostic tests are key to educational equity, then why do so many people have such a viscerally negative reaction when they hear about them? As it turns out, much of this bad reputation is well earned. For generations, diagnostic tests were used not only to produce snapshots of students' relative performance, but also to implement tracking systems that ensured that those snapshots became lasting portraits of inequity.

The most notorious example of this is the extended use of IQ tests. Beginning in the 1920s, IQ tests were used in schools across the country as a means of identifying the academic potential of students and providing them with stratified opportunities based on those results. Students who scored well were often put on the path to college and white-collar jobs, while students who scored poorly were placed in vocational tracks and, likely, on the path to an early exit from the education system. The results of IQ tests almost always confirmed bias about the differential abilities of students based on their race and social class. Those who used these tests gave little consideration to how the content of the tests might say less about a student's biological intelligence than his or her social class and educational opportunities to that point. The fact that students who scored well or poorly would go on to have disparate academic and life outcomes only served to confirm in the minds of many that the initial diagnosis had been correct, their categorically different school experiences notwithstanding.[1]

Even though courts have put limits on some of the most egregious uses, such as when federal courts restricted the use of IQ tests for placement of Black students in special education classes, there are still too many instances in which a standardized test, though not necessarily an IQ test, is used to make an initial tracking determination that students are never able to exit. In other words, diagnostic testing becomes an educational destiny.

When this happens, it is as much a problem with the *use* of the test results by schools and districts as it is with any of the information provided by the tests themselves. As researchers have carefully documented, "tracking" is actually a set of practices that range from sorting students into classrooms based on similar academic skills, to restricting access to advanced curriculum within a single subject, or, in the most severe cases, across all subjects.[2] It's this variation in what schools do with the information provided by standardized tests that determines their appropriateness and value in practice.

Given the stakes involved, it is worth recalling the caution offered by paleontologist and historian of science Stephen J. Gould about treating differences identified by standardized assessments as either natural or permanent. As Gould notes, medical doctors give lots of standardized examinations to patients in order to identify areas of concern—ones often involving genetic predispositions—and the results aren't treated as the end of the story. Instead, they are treated as an impetus for intervention. When someone goes to ophthalmologist and finds she is nearsighted, we don't treat it as a permanent deficiency; we give her a prescription for glasses.[3]

Unfortunately, too often in education our remedies are insufficient and undelivered. Rather than seeing student performance on standardized tests converge across the years of schooling, we see persistent or widening gaps. Little wonder, then, that the tests revealing these gaps become targets of skepticism and criticism. Indeed, this fear about what kind of scores or assessments might be lurking in school files and following students from school to school is why student privacy laws include provisions to allow students to inspect their own educational records.[4]

Going the Distance

The test scores that populate district data systems are not the only ratings that follow students through school. In fact, whereas DIBELS or MAP scores usually travel no further than central office computers, a host of other assessments follow students from high school into college, and from college into graduate school. Somewhat amazingly, these scores are *not* created or disseminated by schools. Instead, they are almost all the products of a single organization: the College Board.

Despite the way that some commentators talk, the fact that a private company is in charge of some of the most consequential standardized tests in American society is not the result of some vast conspiracy. It is, however, a result of the particular history of American education. Our tradition of local control, combined with the limited responsibilities and institutional capacities of state and federal governments, means that key features of the US system have been produced as the result of the coordinated actions of nongovernmental actors. Such actors include organizations like the American Council on Education, which gave us the GED; the Carnegie Foundation, which gave us the Carnegie unit; and the College Board, which is responsible for the SAT and AP examinations.

The College Board is the outgrowth of the College Entrance Examination Board (CEEB), created at the turn of the twentieth century as a way for private colleges in the northeastern United States to standardize their admissions examinations. These early efforts at coordination produced the first version of the SAT, which was administered on a small scale for the first time in 1926. In the wake of the massive expansion of higher education after World War II, the call from colleges, high schools, and students for a more synchronized college admission process moved from a regional to a national concern.

Following a recommendation from President Truman's Commission on Higher Education, several discrete efforts to develop admissions tests coalesced through the creation of the Educational Testing Service (ETS) in 1948. Though joined a decade later by E. F. Lindquist's American College Testing (ACT) organization and its namesake test, for the next half century ETS was the premier organization for the continued research in nascent science of test development. Though the College Board still relies on ETS to produce the actual test, the College Board is the organization that develops policies for the use and administration of these tests.

Though the SAT is the College Board's signature examination, its other flagship product, the AP program, provides an even better view of how, in America's decentralized education system, standardized tests have come to shape the work of schools.

The AP program was initially designed as a way of promoting college-level work in high school—a way of accelerating the advancement of the "best and brightest," while also stimulating their interest and engagement.[5] As with the SAT, the program initially catered to elite, mostly private schools and proved useful to them as a way to demonstrate that they were providing college- and university-level curricular materials to their students. Over time, and in line with broader efforts in public schools to broaden access to honors-level courses, the AP program became increasingly mainstream. The democratization of AP was good for business, and it indicated the extent to which association with a nationally recognized program could overcome local questions about the rigor and quality of course offerings. The lineage of the AP program was even capable of rubbing off on individual schools, as exemplified by the incorporation of AP course-taking statistics into rankings of individual high schools.[6] Over the last decade, the number of high school graduates who have taken at least one AP exam has increased by 43 percent, to the point that 38 percent of high school graduates in 2020–1.2 million students—took at least one AP exam during high school.[7]

Throughout its widespread adoption and expanded course offerings, the AP program remained built around its end-of-course examinations. This created a set of standard scores that could be used to draw comparisons across widely different contexts of schooling. Thus, even though there was no official "AP curriculum," teachers knew that teaching an AP course was first and foremost about getting students prepared for the end-of-term test. In practical terms, this often means that the entire content of the course has to be completed before the examination date, even when there may be weeks remaining in the semester. It is hardly surprising, then, that students in AP classes often believe that passing the AP exam is synonymous with success in these courses.

One reason that high school and college educators have acceded to the growth of the AP program and its suite of exams is that the tests themselves are often much more rigorous than "traditional" standardized tests. Though most utilize multiple-choice questions, they also incorporate open-ended questions that require students to analyze historical documents, compose essays, submit original artwork, or record themselves speaking a foreign language.

Yet, although AP exams come as close to fulfilling the standardized testing proponent's rallying cry of "create tests worth teaching to" as any examinations in widespread use, they still concede huge swaths of pedagogical ground. AP Biology, for instance, is built around students memorizing vast amounts of information, rather than working with lab equipment or conducting experiments. And the AP History examinations, at their best, involve contextualizing a few preselected, closely related documents, rather than engaging in open-ended inquiry.

Teachers and schools must necessarily give up any concerns about deeper learning if they want to participate in the program. Just as importantly, students must embrace the idea that mastery of a subject is synonymous with the results of a standardized test, which most often consists of multiple-choice questions. Commonly, AP teachers will revise students' course grades once the results of their AP exams are returned, adjusting their marks to align with the College Board's scores. In these cases, students are quite literally being told that the only thing to be valued in the course is the portion of knowledge and skills validated by standardized examination.

It is little wonder, then, that students orient themselves increasingly toward tests controlled by organizations outside of their schools. The scores earned on these tests become important pieces of recorded information, which will follow them for years in the future and can continue to shape their academic and professional lives in profound ways. Given the limited predictive validity of these examinations and, in the case of the SAT, ACT, or GRE, given their total disconnect from school curriculum, it is hard to argue that their influence is proportional to their value as informational tools. However flawed a GPA may be as a succinct statement of the totality of a student's work over four years of high school, at least it reflects input from multiple teachers on multiple subjects across multiple years. In this respect, a GPA is a mutual fund compared with the single stock gamble represented by an exam like the SAT or ACT.

Our argument here is not that standardized tests like AP examinations or the SAT provide no important information. On the contrary, they almost certainly offer something valuable, especially when placed alongside other sources of information about a student's educational opportunities and achievements.

But the recognition of this value has resulted in the distortion of educational efforts, both within schools and outside of them. Students spend their summers preparing for the SAT test, parents game the test by paying for their children to take the examination multiple times, and teachers cede large swaths of the curriculum to learning standards devised by the College Board. These are all reasonable responses given the place standardized test scores have come to occupy in our system and the long-term stakes attached to success on these tests. They are also why so many students think of school as fundamentally about testing.

The Educational Panopticon

Much of the impact of standardized testing is on the individual. A student's SAT scores, for instance, affect her and her alone; likewise, a student's score on a diagnostic test affects the resources the school directs towards the student, but not the fundamental operation of the school itself. But the most pervasive testing, which happens annually across K-12 schools in all fifty states—as a part of the measurement and accountability system first introduced by the federal No Child Left Behind Act in 2002—primarily affects the work of schools. NCLB required that states test students annually in grades 3–8 and disaggregate the results by specified subgroups. The law also required schools to report whether they had made adequate yearly progress (AYP) toward securing 100 percent proficiency for all students on the state's standards. A school's failure to reach their AYP target could trigger consequences as serious as state takeover and the removal of staff.

Perhaps not surprisingly, the high-stakes nature of these tests has produced a range of unintended consequences that shape the learning environment and that, ultimately, transform the student experience.[8] Despite these well-documented issues, when NCLB was reauthorized by an overwhelming bipartisan majority as the Every Student Succeeds Act (ESSA), the annual testing requirement was retained, even as the law provided greater flexibility in other areas.

The successive iterations of the United States' signature federal education law highlight the degree to which test scores remain the coin of the realm. Even when the widely decried law was amended, removing the testing requirement was a bipartisan nonstarter. That's because test-based accountability has given state and federal leaders historically unprecedented control over schools. Whatever the limitations of using test scores to monitor school performance, policy elites are entirely dependent on this data; without it, they might have to admit they really don't know how individual schools are doing, which makes them reluctant to relinquish their newly acquired control.[9] Additionally, the public has become accustomed to discussing schools primarily in terms of changes in test scores. Even our conversations about equity and equal access have become inextricably linked to comparing average test scores of different subgroups of students—the so-called achievement gap.

The biggest, and perhaps most obvious, consequence of our testing regime is that state standardized tests give curricular standards power. Each state has a set of curriculum frameworks outlining what students should know and be able to do in particular subjects and at each grade level. In some ways that's a good thing. Such frameworks ensure greater coordination from grade to grade within a school, and from school to school within each state. Yet the high-stakes testing that accompanies many of these curricular standards makes the standards something more akin to a religious text than to an open-ended framework—one must hew closely to the prescribed content or risk punishment. If students are inherently interested in a subject, that may not be a major problem. But for those who aren't, such rigidity can undermine the exploratory, curiosity-driven, and nonlinear nature of authentic learning.

Another negative consequence has been the narrowing of our views of student learning. Though elected officials talk frequently about test results in terms of "student learning," this elides the fact that they are almost always talking about test results in just two subjects: reading and mathematics. As important as these subjects are, they are hardly the whole of learning outcomes we want for our students. Yet virtually the entirety of our discourse about student learning has been collapsed into these two data points. Not surprisingly, schools have taken the cue. Over the last two decades, there has been a well-documented narrowing of the school curriculum. Cuts to writing instruction, science, social studies, art, and music have all limited what students are taught. And many schools have cut recess or made it unrecognizable in an effort to create more instructional time for tested subjects.[10]

Teachers, for their part, have reported less freedom to teach creatively. Even more concerning, there is evidence that teachers have begun viewing their students through the lens of their test scores and are allocating their time and attention accordingly. Students very ncar a proficiency cutoff—so-called bubble kids—are likely to get more attention from their teacher than students further above or below the state benchmarks. This kind of "educational triaging" is a predictable result of accountability policies built around test scores.[11]

Another predictable result of high-stakes testing has been the rise of teaching to the test. Policy leaders would like to think that teachers use the state standards and draw on their deepest pedagogical expertise to develop lesson plans filled with ambitious instruction and multifaceted learning outcomes. Decades of experience, however, have demonstrated that, far more often, teachers begin with the testing documents and follow them closely when thinking about what elements of the standards to emphasize and how to teach them. We might not like this approach, but teachers are well aware that it is highly effective, in part because the tests themselves are so predictable and demand so little from students in terms of creativity and innovative thinking. Indeed, there is suggestive evidence that one reason we see larger test score gains in math than in reading is that standardized math tests are able to measure proficiency levels more precisely. This creates a strong incentive for teachers to spend more time preparing their students for math exams, because these efforts are more likely to be reflected in student test scores.[12] We might wish that teachers would resist or ignore these cues, but it is hard to imagine why they would.

It is only a small step from teaching to the test as a means of preparation to doing full dress rehearsals with the tests themselves. Indeed, many schools engage in regular practice testing as a means of preparing students for end-of-year high-stakes exams. According to a report by the American Federation of Teachers, students in tested grades spend 60 to 110 hours each year on test preparation, and 20 to 50 hours a year taking tests.[13] Though we might decry this use of time and resources, it's far from irrational that schools engage in these practices. Our system and the public at large reward improvements in test scores. So why should they focus on anything else?

Data from state-run standardized testing enables us to bring into comparison schools and students within districts and across states, and such comparisons have become increasingly prominent tools in education policy and public discourse. Our commitment to and reliance on this information is undeniable. Critiques of the perverse incentives created by NCLB proficiency cutoffs resulted not in abandoning test-based accountability but instead the introduction of new forms of test-based accountability measures like student growth measures and teacher value-added scores.[14] Likewise, lawmakers and state officials around the country recently demonstrated that not even a global pandemic is reason enough to stop our annual testing regime.[15] Even when schools themselves have been massively disrupted, the production of standardized test scores must continue apace.

The Good, the Bad, and the Ugly

The gravitational pull of test scores on the attention of policymakers, school officials, and teachers is considerable and has resulted in pulling focus away from a holistic view of student learning and school quality. That said, we would be remiss if we didn't acknowledge the ways in which the pull of standardized test scores has partially aligned with other important policy goals and values like increasing equity in our schools.

Though criticism of standardized testing is well deserved in many respects, there is also general agreement about the value of the low-stakes use of standardized tests as a means of monitoring the need for intervention and support—a potentially important contribution that should not be overlooked. Two decades on, many people have forgotten that many liberals and civil rights groups supported NCLB's annual testing requirements because the law required that results be reported by specific subgroups including racial minorities, English language learners, and students with disabilities. This information has become an essential part of targeted advocacy efforts, as well as of the factual record for lawsuits aimed at securing students' educational rights.[16]

Beyond their use in conversations about educational equity, standardized test scores have also served as a counterbalance to the influence of grades in students' educational trajectories. The same impulse that gives rise to concerns about a single test having too much influence over how schools are perceived also gives rise to concerns that grades themselves represent a very particular and potentially narrow view of student learning. Though discussion of bias in standardized tests gets a great deal more attention, there is considerable evidence that teachers exhibit similar racial and socioeconomic biases that can show up in their assessments of student work or in their recommendations for student placements in honors or gifted programs.[17] In other words, though test scores and grades are imperfect, neither is made less imperfect by removing the other.

There is a reasonable argument to make, then, that removing test scores entirely from consideration simply gives more influence to these other forms of assessment. For instance, there is an ongoing effort to remove or make optional SAT and ACT scores in college applications. While these test scores are correlated with students' socioeconomic status, so are grades. In fact, so is another remaining element of the standard college application: the student essay. As research indicates, both the content and style of college admission essays are correlated with student socioeconomic status—an even stronger relationship than we see between family income and SAT scores.[18] This is not surprising given that, for many students, admissions essays are a collective endeavor—the by-product of multiple rounds of feedback and input from parents, teachers, and college counselors.

In short, test scores may leave a lot to be desired. But there is a reason why they are included in a package of assessments that colleges and universities use to sift through applications. That isn't to say that test scores are always used in responsible ways. However, it does suggest that merely dumping test scores may do as much harm as good. The solution has to be more nuanced than that.

Like grades, test scores may have a place in our assessment system if we can minimize their distorting effects. Until then, however, we should approach them with extreme caution, knowing that any useful tool can also be deployed as a weapon. Only by carefully considering the multiple demands, uses, and audiences for assessment information, as well as the multiple tools available to meet those needs, can we assign tests an appropriate place in our education system.

3

Your Permanent Record

Transcripts are like suitcases. They exist only to transport items from one place to another. The items in question, however, are not the necessities for travel. Instead, they're the record of one's school achievement.

Not surprisingly, transcripts are constrained in what they can hold. And, as they are currently designed, they can hold surprisingly little. Transcripts are intended to be read at a glance—to convey a clear message in short order. Even if shared electronically, they are designed to fit on a standard piece of paper, and ideally should run no more than the length of a single page. Employing a readable typeface, a single page allows only for the listing of course names, the period in which the course was taken, and the grade that was earned. Despite very different learning goals and educational environments, colleges and universities largely replicate this practice. Though they are certain to write the school's name in a large font and emblazon the document with the school crest, a college or university transcript looks virtually identical to those issued by high schools. It lists course titles and grades and includes two modest and concise pieces of additional information: a student's major/minor and any academic honors.

In addition to these school transcripts there are also transcripts produced by testing bodies like the College Board. A student applying to most colleges will have to arrange for a transcript of his test scores—SAT, SAT subject tests, AP examinations—to be sent to a college or university admissions office. Like school transcripts, these reports contain just the basic information: the date, the test name, and the score. In fact, recent efforts have sought to reduce the information even further. Rather than reporting all scores from each test sitting, the reports now often contain only the highest score or the highest combination of sub-scores from across tests. Recent efforts to provide additional information about the student's context—a so-called adversity index—received strong and immediate pushback.[1]

Reporting such weighty information in such a small space requires tremendous compression of information. Imagine packing for the rest of your life—for a trip to Mars—and being handed a suitcase that meets the overhead bin requirements for commercial airlines. Almost everything will need to be left out. Yet only the items that make it into the permanent record, the official transcript, will likely ever be seen. All of one's other accomplishments will need to book separate passage if they want to make the journey.

Recording Learning or Measuring Time?

Everyone who has ever been to school knows that a core function of the transcript is to keep a tally of students' progress toward their degrees. In other words, to keep a record of the total number of credit hours, sometimes called Carnegie units, each student has completed. Just like grades, the credit hour is a form of academic currency, which ultimately gets recorded on the transcript. As a kind of currency, the credit hour puts disparate items—in this case different classes students have taken—into relationship with each other via a single system of value. If everyone took the same classes, it wouldn't be necessary to assign value to different courses or to record the total units at all. But this was precisely the challenge posed by the American education system with its distinct standards, offerings, and curricula.

The variation in course-taking and curricular content meant that neither the courses themselves, nor their content, could serve as the basis for a common educational currency. Instead, the educational currency had to be rooted in some facet of the school experience that was common across schools. The most obvious candidate, and the one utilized in the Carnegie unit, was time.

The idea of using time as the primary unit of measure was not arbitrary or just a matter of convenience. In the nineteenth century, intellectuals started to believe that the mind was like a muscle that could be trained. This analogy was important because it created space for the idea that what was valuable about particular school subjects was not the content itself, though that might be valuable, too, but rather the subject's capacity to strengthen and discipline the mind.

From this view of mental training, it made sense to assign time values (i.e., "academic units") to each class. As the National Education Association's famous 1892 Committee of Ten report explained, "if every subject is to provide a substantial mental training, it must have a time-allotment sufficient to produce that fruit." Each subject available to students within the offered curriculum, the report concluded, "should be approximately equivalent to each other in seriousness, dignity, and efficiency."[2]

Even though psychologists no longer subscribe to this view of mental training, our education system has retained the convention that an hour spent on any academic subject is worth an equal amount of academic credit. This preserves a formal equity across school subjects, assuring that we treat all subjects as the same even as we acknowledge the implausibility of that fact. Although assuming that an hour spent in any of America's roughly 100,000 schools results in an equivalent amount of learning might seem like a stretch, the alternative—allowing each school or district to assign its own value to students' prior classes—would lead to absolute chaos. Better to accept that each hour, in each subject, in each school, is more or less equivalent.

This approach also maintains the curricular choice that we have come to expect in our schools. A student, whether in high school or college, can choose from any number of available courses. And when the student has earned the required number of credits, the school issues a diploma. If a student moves or transfers schools before completing the degree, the credits transfer with her; she picks up at the new institution right where she left off. The result is that a transcript is first and foremost an accounting document.

Critics have long complained about this emphasis, arguing that the use of the credit hour comes at the cost of a more substantive account of learning. Indeed, upon its introduction, educators immediately complained that the Carnegie unit had reduced learning to mere "seat time." Others complained that the Carnegie unit atomized education in a way that undermined its value. As one commentator put it, equating units to degrees was like "purchasing a diploma on the installment plan."[3]

This weakness, though, was also its chief strength. If taken at face value, accepting Carnegie units as the basic measure of schooling massively simplified the administrative work necessary to synchronize a sprawling, decentralized, multilevel school system. The tradition of local control, the inequalities across communities, and the variation among schools made it challenging to standardize anything but the basic structural elements of schooling. The focus on time in the Carnegie unit mirrored the wider development of minimum time requirements for the length of the school day and school year.[4]

Establishing the formal equivalency of classes by recording time makes it easier to understand how the transcript, as an official log of those hours, became the most important record in a nascent school system. Honoring a transcript meant honoring the bureaucratic designations of the education system—namely, the idea that a high school was a high school, and a Latin class was a Latin class. Accepting credits issued by other institutions also meant acknowledging the legitimacy of their place within the growing school system.

Though the Carnegie unit was important in formalizing relationships among the schools that issue and accept them, it still allowed schools to maintain important levels of institutional autonomy. Here the sparseness of the Carnegie unit, and the transcripts on which these units appear, provides an opportunity for schools to require additional information—allowing them to acknowledge the considerable inequalities in the American education system without undermining the system itself. Thus, Stanford University's admissions website can say, "the most important credential for evaluating your academic record is your high school transcript," while still asking for other transcripts containing scores from the ACT, SAT subject tests, and AP exams.[5] This approach carries a simple message to students: without a transcript that shows the right classes—AP and honors wherever possible—a student's application will be rejected at a glance.

Formal Dance

The history of student records, as we detail in Chapter 4, was animated almost entirely by the record-keeping imperatives of school officials and registrars, but these decisions have had important and lasting consequences for students. Though administrators are the official audience for transcripts, students and their families spend far more time thinking about what these permanent records are perceived as saying.

Consider, for instance, the words "honors" or "advanced" on a transcript. Presently, a massive number of students are enrolled in courses bearing such designations. Nearly 40 percent of the high school graduating class of 2017 took at least one Advanced Placement class.[6] And according to polling data, 20–25 percent of students are in honors classes not associated with the AP program, meaning that nearly two-thirds of American students are enrolled in advanced coursework.[7] But what is motivating such massive participation? Is it a desire for more academic challenge?

The emphasis on titles and forms, rather than substance and content, inexorably promotes gamesmanship among students, who see an opportunity to gain an advantage through the careful curation of what appears on their transcripts. A person viewing a transcript has little idea what transpired in such a course. Was it, indeed, more rigorous than the typical version of the course? How rigorous is the alternative, non-honors, offering? How does either course—the honors version or the typical one—compare to other courses with similar titles at other schools? None of this can be determined by reading the transcript.

The uncertainty about course content and rigor provides an opportunity for students—as well as for schools seeking to provide opportunities for their students—to use the "honors" designation to their advantage. Consider one of the most frequent questions received by high school counselors and college admissions officers: "Is it better to get a B in an AP / IB / Honors course or an A in a regular course?"[8] One will note that the framing of the question is fundamentally not about course content or student learning; instead, it is strictly about the trade-in value of various designations. Versions of this hypothetical question about course selection can be found on every website that offers college admissions advice to anxious students and parents. The replies, like this one on CollegeVine.com, emphasize, like the question itself, the importance of how the transcript will "look" to college admissions officers:

> When evaluating your transcript in the admissions process, colleges look not only at your individual grades in each course and GPA, but also the rigor of your curriculum. Having numerous AP, IB, and / or honors courses on your transcript has manifold benefits [including the fact that] your weighted GPA will be higher . . .
>
> If you think you can get at least a B in a rigorous class, you should probably take the class anyway. Colleges want to see that you are challenging yourself and doing as well as possible, because this indicates that you have what it takes to perform well at an elite college and will contribute to the intellectual community.[9]

The above advice is focused chiefly on the arithmetic of transcripts, rather than the content or experience of the courses. The advice on Princeton Review's website states the matter even more plainly, advising students to spot the most appealing arbitrage: "Select AP classes you can ace."[10]

Even if colleges and universities didn't consider student coursework in the admissions process, the nature of transcripts would still encourage students to take honors and Advanced Placement classes. Because the transcript presents all grades in a 4.0 grade point format, it presumes apples-to-apples comparability across classes. Students taking more challenging coursework, then, would naturally have complained to their schools that they were being "punished" with lower GPAs. Many schools and districts, in response, have adopted policies that award an extra "grade point" on the transcript for honors and AP coursework. Thus, a student earning a B in AP Chemistry would receive a 4.0—the grade point equivalent of an A—on her transcript.[11]

The policy in Spokane, Washington, is illustrative, if perhaps not necessarily representative. For honors courses, students receive an extra half point on their transcripts: an A is a 4.5 rather than a 4.0, and a B is a 3.5. In AP courses, they receive a full grade point boost, making an A worth 5.0 on a 4.0 scale.[12] Perhaps not surprisingly, it is now common for many high school students to maintain grade point averages that are higher than the scale itself. A student in Spokane with straight As in all AP classes would have a 5.0 grade point average on a scale that only goes to 4.0.

When these accounting systems get paired with competitive college admissions, the incentives to develop elaborate strategies to maximize one's advantage increase substantially. For instance, in an effort to curb the arms race for more and more AP and honors courses, the University of California (UC) system developed a policy that when calculating a student's GPA, it will only award an additional honors point for a maximum of eight courses during a student's sophomore and junior year. While this may dissuade some students from taking more "extra" APs for the sake of college admission, it also has the effect of encouraging students to ensure that they "max out" the points they receive from their limited number of 5.0 eligible courses. Selecting the "right" AP course for a student—to return to the perennial admissions website question—is crucial for maximizing one's advantage in this system.

Though one might want to take comfort in the idea that the opportunity to experience the rigors of any AP course is valuable all on its own, that does not change the fact that there is still a zero-sum game in operation here. The UC admissions policy states that students whose GPAs place them in the top 9 percent of students in their high schools automatically receive admission to a UC campus. With these stakes, it is hard to fault students who think chiefly about ease-of-grading when considering which classes they should take.

Designations like "honors" and "Advanced Placement" have a particularly golden ring on transcripts. But the names of courses can matter, too, as signaling devices. At many schools, core courses will simply appear as "ENGLISH 9" or "ALGEBRA" on the student transcript. Some schools use these vague titles to their advantage, upgrading a course title to make it appear more rigorous while leaving the course content unchanged. For instance, in the wake of research showing that eighth grade algebra was a useful early predictor of college enrollment, states like California pushed to expand algebra enrollments. Subsequent research into this initiative, however, found that while the state was successful at increasing algebra enrollments, these led to a *decline* in algebra achievement as measured by the state's standardized assessment. As the authors explain, "Algebra (and pre-Algebra) means something different in schools that enroll 90% of eight graders in Algebra than in schools that enroll 40% of eighth graders in Algebra."[13] In other words, many schools were simply re-titling their courses for the sake of appearances.

At the most elite schools, leaders have used their course titles to do something different—showing colleges and universities just how prepared their students are for postsecondary work. At Phillips Academy Andover, for instance, students can enroll in courses like "'The World in Pieces': Poetry and Cinema of the Avant-Garde," "Gender and Power in Tudor England," and "Astrobiology: Life Among the Stars."[14] These courses may be substantively no more challenging than ordinary offerings in art history, social studies, or science. Yet they certainly will appear so on graduating students' transcripts.

These issues are not confined only to high school level course taking. In higher education, however, the considerations around course titles runs in the opposite direction. Rather than looking for impressive-sounding courses to put on their transcripts, many students look for anodyne-sounding classes known to be less demanding. A course listed as "GEOLOGY 110," for instance, may be known widely across campus as "Rocks for Jocks." And "ART HISTORY 201" may be notorious for its relaxing weekly slideshow and easy final exam. Similarly, many savvy students know that a "Directed Reading" or "Independent Study" on the transcript is a cryptic black box, nearly indecipherable by anyone examining their records. Such customized courses, arranged with the consent of instructors, can often be incredibly valuable educationally speaking, as well as quite challenging. But because they are arranged on an individual basis, and because they are given a generic catchall title, they are ripe for abuse.

Students game their transcripts in other ways, as well. One strategy is to distribute effort across courses to maximize one's GPA. As one study found, students chose to take courses on a pass / fail basis either to devote more time to other (graded) courses or to protect their GPAs.[15] Another strategy is to drop classes that students anticipate low grades in. Knowing that their transcripts will not show a record for classes that they never technically took, students pay careful attention to "add / drop" deadlines. Similarly, students are attuned to "grade-basis" deadlines, when they can opt to take a class for a letter grade or simply on a pass / fail basis. These deadlines often coincide with important exams, like midterms, leading students to make major decisions either without information about their as-yet-ungraded performance or based only on the results of a single test. To be clear, there is nothing wrong with students engaging in this kind of behavior, and it makes sense given the perceived high stakes of a bad grade undermining plans to apply to, say, medical school. But the fact that student behavior is animated by these considerations at all highlights the extent to which learning can become a secondary, tertiary, or even more distant consideration.

Perhaps the best way to gild a transcript is with an award designation. In higher education, Latin honorifics—cum laude ("with honors"), magna cum laude ("with high honors"), and summa cum laude ("with the highest honors")—are perhaps the clearest way of indicating one's ranking in a graduating class. In most cases, such designations are based exclusively on grade point averages, using either one's relative standing among peers or the attainment of a pre-specified GPA. In the University of Massachusetts system, if a student's GPA places her in the top 25 percent of the graduating class, she will receive "cum laude" designation. To earn "magna cum laude" and "summa cum laude," she must finish in the top 10 percent or top 5 percent, respectively.[16] Either mode of calculation incentivizes students, especially those on the cusp, to calculate what grades they need to earn particular honors and make decisions about which classes to take and how hard to work.

In short, the commitment to the formal elements of transcripts that make them conducive to academic accounting also allow local economies of insider knowledge to flourish. All but the shrewdest outsider will gain from a transcript only the most cursory understanding of student academic preparation. Students know this, and they use such opacity to their advantage.

Major Problems and Minor Mistakes

In addition to listing grades, college and university transcripts identify students' majors, minors, and other official certifications. The purpose of listing this information on a transcript, as well as on the diploma, is not just a formality. The listed majors and minors are intended to speak to what a student knows and can do. Yet they are inherently unable to offer any substantive information about a student's interest in or aptitude for a discipline or subject. Instead, they offer only the name of the degree pathway.

Even so, this information sends a powerful signal. Students know that among the first questions they will be asked by future employers is about their selected major. The major conveys an important message about a student's academic interest and professional intents. Afraid that a single message isn't sufficient, students at many universities try to reinforce or supplement it by racking up one, two, or even three minors before they graduate. For many, the determination is made not because of any inherent interest, but because enough credits have been accumulated in a particular subject area that it seems foolish not to pick up the credential. A student who takes four courses in in a subject but neglects the crucial last one necessary to declare a minor will have missed out on an important opportunity to signal to future employers or graduate school admissions committees.

These messages are often explicitly communicated to students by academic advisors. For instance, one handbook explains the selection of a minor as a simple matter of angling for advantage: "Another good reason for selecting a minor is that it can give the student a competitive advantage in the job market or as a candidate for graduate school. For example, if you plan on using your psychology major as an entry into the helping professions, a minor in a foreign language that enhances your speaking and writing proficiency can make you very attractive to agencies that serve immigrant communities."[17] As this advice makes clear, underscoring an interest by completing a minor declares an intent and preserves the signal for posterity. The more uncertain the job prospects are for students in a given field, the more motivated they may be to formalize their interest in a variety of subjects.

In the earliest days of American higher education, students all took the same set of courses; as a result, there were no majors to speak of. This changed with the relaxing of course requirements. The goal in doing so was to allow for the deeper pursuit and development of students' interests. The elective system was intended to allow each student, in the words of Charles Eliot, to pursue "the highest development of his own peculiar faculty." A system run on choice, he argued, would give "free play to natural preferences and inborn aptitudes," foster "enthusiasm for a chosen work," and relieve professors of having to compel students to complete an "unwelcome task."[18] Pursuit of learning and mastery, not credential seeking, was the original goal of allowing students the flexibility to select their own paths through postsecondary education.

The idea of the "major" as a formal designation first appeared at Johns Hopkins University in 1877, and from there quickly spread across the country.[19] At Johns Hopkins, students were required to choose major and minor courses from among subjects in six different departments: French, German, math, chemistry, biology, and physics. Roughly two years of study were required for the major program, and one for the minor. Other colleges and universities built on this basic model and made it their own.

Over time, the early interest in allowing students to deepen their understandings of a discipline has given way to majors as something more akin to tokens. This is not because students are opposed to the idea of developing expertise, but rather because they have responded rationally to the incentives presented by the transcript. As a result, the most popular major among college undergraduates is business. Today, American college students are nearly ten times more likely to major in business than in English, and forty times more likely to major in business than in philosophy.[20] Twice as many students major in business as they do in all six of Johns Hopkins University's original majors combined.

The compression of information that confounds efforts to parse the individual lines on a transcript are no less challenging when those entries are aggregated into an official major. What exactly does it mean when a student majors in business? What is it that this student can do that distinguishes him or her from the economics major at another school or the business administration major at his own school? At some schools it might mean a greater attention to theory, more coursework in mathematics, or a more intense focus on practical, applied skills. Without knowing more contextual information about the specific school and individual department—information never contained on the transcript itself—one would never know for sure. In fact, it would be hard to say for certain what makes the business major different from his or her counterparts in the English or philosophy departments.

Students know exactly how to play this game. As one research team found, the top reason for choosing a business major was career interest and job opportunities; least influential was instructional quality.[21] The same logic applies for students who imagine their next step after college is graduate school. Consider, for instance, the proliferation of "pre-law" and "pre-med" programs, which are explicitly about signaling to future admissions committees that applicants have what it takes. In fact, the pressure to major or minor in the "right" subject to signal one's interest in graduate study has gotten so strong that some graduate schools have made *relieving* these constraints a primary selling point of their programs. The medical school at Mount Sinai, for instance, allows students to apply for admission in their sophomore year of college, freeing them from the obligation to pick one of the traditional medical school feeder majors.

To be clear, there is nothing inherently wrong with schools requiring students to have some structure to their course taking. Taking thirty-two random courses, all at the introductory level, might have its benefits in terms of breadth. But it would certainly come at the expense of any depth. Colleges and universities, then, strive for some balance—usually by requiring students to take a range of basic requirements across departments, requiring them to select a major, and leaving room for the selection of electives. Yet because of the way colleges and universities send long-haul messages to future employers and graduate programs about students' academic work, the selection of majors and minors exerts a massive influence on the way students view their work in postsecondary education. A time that should be about intellectual exploration and deepening interests can often be reduced to a set of strategic calculations and signaling attempts.

A Bottleneck for Reform

The need to record student achievement on a school transcript has created a bottleneck for a wide variety of efforts to reform the way student learning is assessed. The limited format of transcripts—lists of course titles and grades—already presents a barrier to effective communication about student achievement. But the fact that it has become a universal standard makes it difficult to alter assessment practice in a way that might disrupt the centrality of grades and test scores.

These critiques are neither new nor novel. In fact, the recurring efforts to reform this system demonstrate how deeply embedded transcripts are in institutional, educational, and cultural practices. Writing in 1940, one author observed that "Marking systems which use letter grades or numbers tend to be arbitrary. They are inflexible and allow little opportunity for suggestions as to possible improvement." Additionally, the author noted, "Letter or number grades suffer the fault of 'covering up' weaknesses as well as points of strength." In narrative reports, by contrast, "there is something personal and human . . . The parent can get a real picture of what is happening at school."[22] These complaints gave rise to experimentation with more subjective forms of grading. Seeking to push back on the descriptive austerity of letter grades, schools in the 1950s and 1960s began experimenting with qualitative descriptions of student progress. Teachers in these schools adopted end-of-course narratives, in lieu of grades, on an experimental basis. Yet an entrenched standard would be difficult to overcome. Perhaps chiefly, there is the challenge of parental expectations. Having received letter grades themselves, parents would likely expect to see such marks for their children. A 1955 article titled "What's All the Fuss about Report Cards?" described a range of alternatives to A–F grading, and speculated that readers might react with admiration or, equally likely, with "frustration, bewilderment, anger."[23] While the article noted the benefits of narrative reports, specifically, that they are "flexible and diagnostic, providing a maximum of truly useful information," it also flatly stated that narratives "take too much time and effort to prepare." Moreover, it noted, narratives "can be hard to understand" with regard to a child's class rank or relative performance.[24]

The issue of interpretation—understanding the meaning of non-letter grades—is trickier than it might appear and underscores the particular challenges of innovating on the transcript. We now take for granted that the information on transcripts can be treated as interchangeable. Course titles and the grades that indicate performance in those courses are treated as academic currency that will be honored in full should a student transfer schools or advance from one level of school to the next. Narrative grades, while providing more detailed information about school performance, also introduce new forms of ambiguity that can be disruptive and, ultimately, counterproductive. (We describe these at greater length in Chapter 7.)[25]

One such ambiguity is about the time necessary to interpret and understand the information contained in a narrative evaluation. As one pair of authors wrote in 1976, "Descriptive evaluations are too long and too complicated for some time-beleaguered admissions officers to read."[26] Because they cannot be handled by the standard administrative procedures, special arrangements need to be made to translate this information into standard forms. Whether this translation results in the effective use of the additional information available is difficult to know.

The second challenge is that the narrative, for all its descriptive content, often omits the piece of information that is most salient to the person reading it: How does this student compare with the others in her class? When teachers provide grades, they are providing a measure of relative standing—students with grades of A or A-minus did the best, students with grades of B-plus or B did slightly less well, and so on. Without that clear rank-order provided by the teacher, narrative grades demand that some future reviewer make the relevant determination even though they, having never met the student, are in a much worse position to do so.

Mostly, however, the nature of the transcript has precluded alternative approaches like narrative assessment. Even in those dwindling number of cases where schools have persisted with narratives, the power of the transcript is obvious. Alverno College in Milwaukee, for instance, does not issue traditional A–F grades. As the college handbook states: "a single letter doesn't tell you whether you have mastered the content for a course and know how to apply the theories in the real world."[27] Still, Alverno exists within a larger system that demands transcripts. And insofar as that is the case, Alverno's approach would place its graduates at a disadvantage by denying them the form of currency used by other institutions. In response, Alverno has capitulated by creating a shadow transcript for students—one that is shared only by request, and which uses typical A–F grading. As the college puts it: "We recognize and value the documented educational significance of narrative feedback and self-assessment to student learning. We also want to open opportunities for our students in competitive scholarships, internships, employment, and advanced degrees where narrative transcripts are not easily communicated or recognized. To facilitate these opportunities, faculty submit grade equivalencies to the registrar at the end of each semester."[28]

States and districts that have tried to adjust their evaluation formats have run into similar problems. Maine, for instance, recently made a push to move from letter grading to competency-based assessment. The upshot of this shift, as one superintendent explained, was to make things more focused on student performance: "Parents may ultimately stop seeing report cards with A, B, or C grades on it and instead start seeing what it is that their students can do."[29] That was the theory at least. In practice, districts found that even when portfolios were created, the need to record something on a transcript restricted the kind of information conveyed. Yes, the numbers recorded—1–4, rather than A–F—more explicitly corresponded to levels of competency, but the change was more in degree than in kind. Even still, families in Maine worried about whether colleges in other states would know what to do with a transcript marked with 3s and 4s. As one parent put it, "The one thing [my son] stressed about was the GPA. 'How does this 4 or 3 on a paper correlate to a GPA and how much money is a [college] gonna give me?' He stressed about that because he worked hard to be where he is today in his class."[30]

Such examples underscore just how much pressure the present assessment regime exerts on teachers, schools, and systems at all levels to stay in line. A change in one place is only sustainable if the rest of the system is willing to accept it. Whether students who present alternative transcripts are actually at a disadvantage is less important than the overwhelming perception that they are.

Banking and Bean Counting

As with grading more generally, the limited information contained on a transcript does provide a bureaucratic equity that is useful in counteracting some of the inequality in the American school system. Even though we know that not all algebra classes are equivalent and not all schools that offer algebra courses are the same, nearly all schools, states, and universities honor the information printed on a transcript. Though some elite schools make a point of deviating from the norm, for most schools recording less information emphasizes the surface-level similarity across all schools and minimizes the extent to which the inequalities that pervade our education system appear on student transcripts. This does not mean that a savvy admissions officer cannot infer shades of difference on transcripts from different schools with different reputations, but when it comes to recording and calculating GPAs, this formal, bureaucratic equity is maintained.

There is also something to be said about the clear communication that comes from the ordinal ranking of grades—that is, by showing who came in first, second, third, and so on. While narrative grades might provide more information and more descriptive accounts of students and their work, the interpretation and commensuration of competing narrative evaluations can require a full exegesis of the document. How should one weigh the statement "I highly recommend this student" against another that says "I recommend this student without qualification"? Are "passionate" and "hardworking" simply euphemisms for "not the best or brightest"? After reading several hundred letters containing several hundred more adjectives, one can sympathize with those who argue for the succinct, if cold, speech of simple letter grades.

Though many lament that a single bad grade on a transcript will haunt a student in perpetuity, a word should also be said for the other side of this proposition. A hard-earned grade exists permanently on a student's transcript and remains in the institution's safekeeping in perpetuity. If, in ten years, an alumnus decides to go to graduate school, his college registrar's office will still be able to produce a transcript of everything that was accomplished a decade prior. In this case, too, the simplicity of the message is an asset. A decade later, few people would like to stand on a set of work products or written attestation that no longer reflects their ability to write or engage critically. Though it is easy to reflexively assume that more is more—that more detail and more description will invariably benefit students—the enduring, austere simplicity of the transcript should mediate this instinct. The "missing" information often accrues to the student's benefit. Eliminating the transcript in favor of something longer and more complicated could easily do more harm than good.

The transcript is a medium for carrying some of the most important information produced by K–12 schools and postsecondary institutions. Over a century, it has developed to work in tandem with letter grades and test scores, conveying the information necessary to allow students to move through a vast and decentralized education system. In this role, it is well adapted and highly efficient. That efficiency does not come without a cost, however. Students and schools can take advantage of simple descriptions to give the impression of rigor and maximize their GPAs for the sake of getting ahead. And though the transcript is not the only reason that students engage in this behavior, it certainly abets them in these efforts.

While it's easy to decry the problems and limitations of the transcript, it is much harder to develop alternatives. As we discuss in Chapter 7, many reform efforts have targeted the information that appears on the transcript—arguing for the replacement of grades with descriptive narratives, for instance, or for the elimination of honors courses in favor of de-tracking—but these ideas have rarely expanded beyond local experiments. The recurring challenge that these efforts inevitably face is that any change in the way grading occurs must also consider the way the message is conveyed.

PART II

A World of Scores

How We Got Here and Why We're Stuck

4

Tools of Necessity

*I*n the long arc of the history of education, grades, test scores, and transcripts are relatively recent inventions. That isn't because such tools were beyond the conceptual or technological capacities of earlier societies. Instead, they weren't invented because they simply weren't necessary.

It might be hard to imagine a school in which the results of assessments are not recorded. Even harder to imagine is a school where the results of assessment are kept secret, known only to teachers until the highest scoring student is revealed at graduation.[1] As strange as it may seem, this is the world that existed for decades in the United States. In order to understand how schools could operate under such different parameters and without such seemingly commonsense tools at their disposal, we have to think more deeply about the relationship between the goals of schooling and the capacities of grades, ratings, and rankings as assessment technologies.

One reason that such technologies were unnecessary is that there was no formal schooling system prior to about two hundred years ago. Education existed, certainly, but was handled chiefly on a relational basis. The family of an aspiring student would hire a teacher to offer instruction in a variety of fields. Student and teacher would develop an intimate relationship, and the teacher would pace the instruction in accordance with the development of his charge. There was no reason to formally record this progress, except for posterity, and no reason to formally report it. The number of interested parties was small and the communication could remain informal.[2]

Hiring a teacher was expensive, but the greatest financial sacrifice made by families choosing to educate their children was in keeping them out of the labor market. Moreover, the investment in education was unlikely to pay financial dividends. As a result, students tended to be an elite and self-selected group, bound to inherit the social status of their families.

Families without the means to hire a tutor could also acquire education for their children, perhaps most commonly by contracting them out as apprentices. In exchange for labor, a master craftsman would teach his apprentice to earn a living in the trade, and sometimes also to read, write, and do basic math. The success of these educational endeavors was proved not by grades or test scores, but by whether the apprentice could ultimately earn a living in the trade. Indeed, craftsmen who didn't fulfill the terms of these agreements sometimes found themselves sued by parents for breach of contract.[3]

Whether young people were studying with private tutors or working as apprentices, there was no need to communicate about their performance across broad stretches of space and time. To the extent that there was communication beyond the family, it was done on an individual basis. Letters of introduction served as a key conduit, and the few academies or schools that did exist either conducted their own examinations of potential students or accepted students by family reputation and ability to pay. None required formal marking. And there was no point in anything resembling a transcript. After all, what use would it serve?

We don't have to romanticize this world to recognize that it had some desirable, even laudable elements. Because learning was costly and required effort to procure, it was rarely done without a specific goal or purpose in mind at the outset. Communication about progress was rich and proximate—readily evident to both parents and students.

But there's also quite a bit *not* to like about these practices. This was a radically unfair and unequal world—a world in which entire populations of students were excluded from the opportunity to get an education, and there was comparatively little opportunity to get ahead based on educational achievement. An individual child's access to education was dependent on the resources of their parents and the opportunities available in their communities. Education was rarely a pathway for advancement except for those who were already near the top of social and economic hierarchies. Intelligence and hard work, despite some notable exceptions, weren't enough. Moreover, it was an exclusive world in which most never got more than basic literacy.

Today, inequality still shapes the opportunities afforded to young people. And our schools all too often provide education on unequal terms. Yet it is also true that large sections of the population and considerable government resources are committed to improving educational access and quality. The need to document and track the product of education stems in large part from these societal commitments. Communicating to a widening public and monitoring schools at a growing scale place a premium on standardized forms of assessment. Distilling student learning to numbers that can easily be ranked, compared, and combined to produce still other measures has become the standard response to this challenge. Though quantifying student learning in this way often creates problems we are all familiar with, it also provides the tools to make good on our educational promises. Thus, making sure we understand the problems that grades, ratings, and rankings were created to solve must be central to any consideration of how we might do better in the future.

Pre-History: Early Experiments with School Evaluations

In 1785, Yale president Ezra Stiles recorded in his diary the results of an examination he had conducted of the college's students. Among the fifty-eight tested, there had been "Twenty Optimi, sixteen second Optimi, twelve Inferiores (Boni), ten Perjores."[4] Stiles gave the scores and determined the rankings.

But what had prompted those strange categories?

Stiles, it seems, was mimicking a classification scheme that had been introduced at Cambridge University. Early in the eighteenth century, the university established the Mathematical Tripos examination—a multiday academic tournament, in which students were ranked and re-ranked after each day of testing.[5] As the tournament advanced, students faced tougher opponents and more difficult questions. The winners earned major distinctions; the highest scorer received a portion of the university's endowment for the rest of his life.[6]

Why was the Tripos introduced at Cambridge? The examination was the result of organizational factors within the university, as well as a response to evolving ideas of merit and distinction. Both sets of considerations will sound familiar to the modern reader. The introduction of an examination system served as a check on the autonomy of the individual colleges that made up the university: by forcing the students of each college to compete against each other in a standardized assessment, Cambridge created a public mechanism of accountability. The reputational stake of a college whose students never fared well in the competition might raise uncomfortable questions.

If the format of the examination was dictated by college structure, the content of the examination was dictated by the practical challenges associated with carrying out such an examination. The emphasis on mathematics, as opposed to other traditional subjects like natural philosophy or Latin, was largely a function of the subject lending itself to more precise, "objective" evaluation. Indeed, participants complained about such a narrow focus. One, for instance, observed that "all other excellencies . . . are quite overlooked and neglected: the solid learning of Greece and Rome is a trifling acquisition; and much more so, every polite accomplishment."[7] An examination based on mathematics, however—even if it was narrow in its design—would not leave room for disagreement about the right answer to the questions.

Despite the elaborate rules and choreography around the Tripos, the results were only of consequence to a minority of students. Students from aristocratic families, who viewed the attempt to establish minute distinctions among peers as unseemly, were expressly exempted from participation in the examinations. It was primarily those students lacking useful social connections who were most interested in the honors and prestige available through the examination system, as it opened the possibility of earning a living as a private tutor or taking up a position within the university itself. Cambridge also saw value in promoting the idea of merit at a time when the university's opponents in parliament were raising questions about what the country received in exchange for the university's continued autonomy.[8]

Presidents and faculty at America's growing number of colleges and universities took this British idea and adapted it to the American context. After the American Revolution, as ideas about merit shifted, colleges were looking to retire old practices that often involved publishing ranked lists of students based entirely on more traditional British-style social distinctions such as the perceived prestige of their families or the prestige of their fathers' professions.

Replacing these older distinctions with divisions rooted more firmly in academic performance and social conduct seemed an appropriate basis for distinguishing an elite in the United States.[9] Systematic assessment of students in American colleges got a substantial boost in the 1820s, when Sylvanus Thayer, superintendent at West Point, instituted a numerical marking system in which each class was assigned a weight (not all classes at that time were weighted equally) and a cadet's performance in each course would be graded. Given the sensitivity to both favoritism and partisanship in the nascent American officer corps, the mechanical operation of Thayer's system, which provided a ranked list of graduates that would be used to order their commissions, was a welcome innovation. The reliance on systematic rules, rather than the whims of individual examiners, was widely seen as a desirable way to make evaluation, and the distinctions conferred on students as a result, fairer and more rational. As a consequence, the system was widely imitated across higher education in the United States.[10]

At Harvard, where the practice of ranking students by family status had long since been retired, President Charles Eliot created a

Latin honor system that divided students based on their performance into three categories: cum laude, magna cum laude, and summa cum laude.[11] At Yale, faculty had misgivings about conferring such titles on students—a practice that struck them as antidemocratic—and instead experimented with a 0 to 4 grading system. Wary both of titles and of the corrupting spirit of competition, individual student performance was recorded in a "Book of Averages" that was kept secret until graduation. Only at graduation would students learn who ranked at the top of the class—an honor that came with the right to deliver a speech at commencement. Such moments of personal recognition and distinction among peers were highly prized by American college students.

These new practices seemed to provide a sounder basis for conferring praise and making distinctions among students. And soon, allowing students to distinguish themselves through academic achievement became what "real" colleges and universities did. That said, some adoption was the result of a clear need to maintain order on campuses and control over the student body. Unlike tutors employed by individuals and operating inside their clients' homes, colleges and universities schooled their pupils at some distance from parents and families. Students recognized this and often behaved accordingly, frequently testing campus boundaries. Throughout the nineteenth century, American college students developed a robust social and extracurricular culture. This culture was sometimes scholastic in character—organized around literary societies, for instance—but just as often was characterized by an open disinterest, if not outright opposition, to the educational goals of the faculty. In 1860, the faculty of Rutgers recorded their first experience with the "slope," in which all the members of a professor's class would get up, leave class, and go down the hill (the slope) away from the college. The willingness of an entire class of students to remove themselves, one by one, from class in the middle of a lecture, served as a not-so-subtle reminder of the limited pull professors had over their students.[12]

Many colleges responded by incorporating behavior into students' grades and informing parents of student conduct. As one might expect for a military institution, West Point's marking system, as designed by Thayer, included a measure of personal conduct within each course grade. In the 1820s, Harvard began sending reports to parents indicating academic and behavioral conduct, including whether students had attended chapel.[13] And at William and Mary, faculty reports listed four categories to distinguish students: the "first in their respective classes"; those who were "orderly, correct and attentive"; those who made "very little improvement"; and those who learned "little or nothing . . . on account of excessive idleness." The college shared this information with parents and guardians, along with notes on the propriety of student conduct.[14]

These ideas about assessment, which began in the nation's postsecondary institutions, diffused throughout the system and down into the K-12 level. Graduates of American colleges were a natural source of teachers for the many elementary and secondary schools that began to crop up with increasing frequency throughout the nineteenth century. Additionally, many of the private academies that were founded in this period were in direct competition with local colleges for paying students and, therefore, tended to imitate their practices. Though its students lived at home under the supervision of their parents, Central High School in Philadelphia joined the practice of many American colleges in including behavior along with academic performance in student grading. The spirit of competition and the desire for recognition among one's peers and community, referred to at the time as "the spirit of emulation," and which was such a central element of collegiate life, was a key pedagogical principle of many academies and early common schools.[15]

A "Healthy Competition"

Americans of the nineteenth century increasingly wanted an education for their children. Looking for a reliable way to secure social position, status, and white-collar employment for their children in a rapidly changing society, middle-class Americans increasingly invested in schools and their children's education.[16] But as demand grew, and as schools expanded, it became clear that children did not always want that education for themselves.

The pedagogical concern with student motivation was common in the mid-nineteenth century. At the dawn of the Civil War, the former principal of Chauncy-Hall School in Boston wrote in "Letters to a Young Teacher" that educators must immediately establish a "merit roll" and inspire students to compete for "front rank." Doing so, he argued, might produce something resembling cooperation.[17] In developing this desire among students to compete for recognition of their merit, schools had to engage in a delicate balance. Emulation could produce a healthy competition spurring achievement, revealing those worthy of imitation, and raising the bar of distinction for those who followed. At the same time, however, critics charged that such a spirit could produce unwholesome feelings of envy and resentment, as well as an emphasis on individual advancement at the expense of the collective good.[18]

Such concerns spurred efforts to motivate students to focus on academic tasks, not for the sake of distinction, but for that of their educational value. In 1831, the *Annual Report of the President of Harvard University* asserted that "the best assurance for the continued and unremitted attention of students to their exercises . . . [is] the certainty that at every recitation each individual will be examined; and that the estimate of scholastic rank must depend, not upon occasional brilliant success, but upon the steady, uniform, and satisfactory performance of each exercise."[19] Students, in other words, might apply themselves a bit more to their studies if they knew there would be a lasting record of their performance.

This notion of steady, continual work at school led to a breakthrough innovation: the report card. The technology was rooted in a critique of prior evaluative practice, which emphasized the ultimate reward of public praise, rather than the steady work required to secure it. Horace Mann, for instance, wrote in his ninth annual report as secretary of education in Massachusetts that "if superior rank at recitation be the object, then, as soon as that superiority is obtained, the spring of desire and of effort for that occasion relaxes."[20] In making this observation, Mann wasn't suggesting that such rankings should be eliminated. Instead, he believed that they should be conducted more frequently, via a series of monthly reports. Mann likened these reports to a merchant's ledger, illustrating how short-term investments obtained profitability over months and years. In this way, students would come to understand learning as an endeavor with a much longer horizon than implied by the traditional organization of school assessments, which were built around ephemeral competition and daily exercises. Thus, Mann argued, a student might come to understand that "his mind will be submitted for inspection not only on its bright side, but on all the sides; and that it will be useless for him to expect to shine on that occasion with only a radiant beam of light thrown across it here and there, while wide intervals of darkness lie between."[21]

The extent to which the report card was widely understood by teachers as an explicit motivation and spur for students is suggested by an 1862 ad published in *The Connecticut Common School Journal*. The ad from the Holbrook School Apparatus Company announced the sale of "New and Beautiful School Incentives; Rewards of Merit, Teachers' Tokens, Reports, Certificates, Mottoes, &c." The report cards were available in two formats—monthly and weekly reports—and, again underscoring their use as a showy token, were offered in "various patterns and printed in several colors."[22]

Not only did report cards provide a new form of motivation and more effectively communicate the values that reformers like Mann sought to establish in the schools, but they also proved more effective at communicating with parents. Prior to the invention of report cards, parents, and citizens more generally, were treated to a yearly exhibition in which students would complete public recitations and answer (preplanned) questions from their teachers. Though exhibitions were popular and considered major events in the life of a community, they were also far from ideal modes of communication.[23]

Through a well-rehearsed, well-drilled performance, the tax-paying citizens of a community might see that their local teacher ran a tight ship and was firmly in control of his charges. Yet such presentations offered very little information to most parents about what their own children had learned. Report cards, by contrast, offered a regular and direct line of communication with parents and students about student academic performance.

Indeed, the practice of providing regular report cards to parents came to be seen as part of the standard record-keeping necessary for running a school. Educators and administrators sought to devise ways to streamline these practices, as in the case of a school principal who developed an integrated three-part record-keeping system, which, according to one practitioner-oriented journal, was an "ingenious device" that "saves much time and labor in making out records." Specifically, the system allowed teachers to track "daily attendance, conduct, and recitation"; maintain a "permanent record of monthly averages"; and supply "a monthly report-card for the inspection of parents."[24] Even if most parents were not in a position to intervene in their children's education, the communication between teacher and parent was nevertheless important in solidifying the bonds between families and this newest of social institutions: public schools.

Exerting Control

Grades may have been useful for motivating students and communicating with families. But they weren't particularly useful from the perspective of evangelizers like Horace Mann, who hoped to build a network of what he called "common schools" for American children—the foundation of today's public education system. As the nascent public education system grew in size, and received more in state appropriations, advocates understood that communicating to the broader public would be crucial in winning their approval. In addition to annual exhibitions that allowed the public to see for themselves the work their schools had done in educating the local youth, school officials also began issuing annual reports describing school activities. Here, too, Horace Mann was a major innovator. In addition to reporting basic statistical information about things like the number of students enrolled and total expenditures, Mann decided to provide narrative accounts of school activities in his annual reports starting in 1837. Presaging the tension between qualitative and quantitative accounts of schooling, the two accounts—one narrative, one statistical—would be published as two distinct parts of the annual report. This became the standard format for annual reports by school officials across the country and a primary vehicle for generating support for public schools.[25]

Though annual reports were effective ways to inform the public in some regards, they could not speak to questions about the relative quality of schooling. These questions became increasingly important as expenditures for schooling consumed larger and larger portions of state and local budgets. They also became of particular interest to state officials like Mann who were interested in raising the professionalism, quality, and efficiency of schools. State officials like Mann found the traditional means of school inspection—public exhibitions or direct inspection by officials—provided very weak forms of oversight. While some local officials might be able to visit every school and develop face-to-face relationships with principals and teachers, this was not possible at the state level nor even in large urban school systems.

The first standardized tests were employed explicitly as a means of providing officials the capacity to conduct their inspections in a uniform way and from afar. Bringing schools under uniform inspection and, therefore, in direct comparison with each other, also had the added benefit—at least as district and state officials saw it—of shifting the balance of power away from teachers and principals. These dynamics were evident in the very first use of written standardized tests in American schools.

Horace Mann and his colleague Samuel Gridley Howe introduced standardized tests to American common schools as part of a larger effort aimed at showing how the current organization of schools, curriculum, and modes of instruction deserved scrutiny and were in need of radical reform. By printing the results of examinations in the local papers, Mann and his fellow reformers hoped to strengthen their case for reform, influence, and greater oversight.[26] Sure enough, Mann's tests suggested that the considerable pride Bostonians had in their schools was misplaced. The standardized test results showed that even Boston's top students had only managed to average 30 percent on the examination, and that their scores were lower than those in some surrounding areas. What followed would sound familiar to any contemporary watcher of public education: newspapers printed lists of the best and worst performing schools; some teachers of particularly low performing students were fired; and the test scores were cited in public debates as evidence of a school system in "decline."[27]

Though Mann and his colleagues hoped to put the issue into "black and white," the results of these early tests hardly settled the matter. They did, however, introduce a new tool for school officials and policy elites seeking to understand (and critique) the work of schools. At the time of Boston's first foray into standardized tests, Mann predicted that "the mode of examination *by printed questions and written answers* will constitute a new era in the history of our schools."[28] And for the most part he was right.

The idea that students and schools could be brought into comparison by quantifying student learning using standardized tests, and that this was a sensible way to compare what people recognized as otherwise non-standardized systems, quickly took hold of the public's imagination. As one early twentieth-century commentator mocked (echoing Mann's initial critique): "If one could read all the small-town papers of any given state for one year, he would probably find three fourths of them claiming that their home town had the best schools in the state." These empty assertions, the author argued, stood in contrast to the "new" method requiring a superintendent to put speculation aside and compare his own students' achievement with those attending school elsewhere, doing so "by means of a standard test."[29]

It was not just reformers or the public at large that had an interest in the results of standardized tests. Exam results were increasingly used by colleges and universities attempting to establish the relative performance of students who graduated from different high schools. Traditionally, colleges had sent individual professors out to assess the academic preparation of area students. But while standardized to a degree—it was the same professor passing judgment on a group of students—the variation in content and rigor of these examinations differed from professor to professor.

With the advent of standardized tests, however, postsecondary institutions increasingly moved to systematize the content and form of their entrance examinations. As one college official put it: "Our aim has been in part to contribute to the solution of an education problem. Students, on entering college as freshmen, are a heterogeneous lot. Some come from first-class high schools, others from poor ones. Some have already acquired in their homes habits of accuracy or of perseverance, others are not so fortunate. Some know how to study, others have been carried along without much effort of their own."[30] In other words, standardized tests and the quantified results they produced would create comparability across students and contexts.

As the role for standardized tests grew, many would claim that they had become a wellspring of pernicious effects on schools and students: introducing the phenomenon of test-prep, narrowing the curriculum around tested content, and generating concern about the effects of "over-study" on children. Even so, proponents countered that standardized test scores offered definitive and easy-to-communicate evidence about student performance, which was so lacking in prior eras. As the author of a 1922 text wrote, "The scores on standardized tests supply to the pupil's goal just this definiteness. When such scores are represented by a simple graph, say with one line showing the given pupil's attainment in these tests and another line the attainment of the average American child of this age or grade who has taken these tests, then the pupil has his strong and weak points set before him in a manner that is perfectly definite and objective."[31]

Sources of Comparison

Horace Mann was right in his prediction that, once introduced into American education, standardized tests would never cease to be a defining feature of the system. But even as school officials and reformers found new uses for standardized tests, they did not displace the use or value of grades for teachers and students. The older argument that a student's performance in a class—as expressed in grades issued by his teacher and memorialized on a report card or transcript—provided motivation for students to do their best work still held sway. As one commentator explained, though the "marking systems of today are fraught with innumerable weaknesses and inconsistencies, their most loyal adherents cannot deny; on the other hand, they do serve as a spur to the laggard, even their most outspoken opponents must admit."[32]

For its critics, the most concerning weaknesses of the grading system was its persistent lack of uniformity. Although grades had become a relatively typical feature of schools by the end of the Civil War, no standardization in their form had emerged by the early twentieth century. Some schools or districts employed lettered systems, others percentage systems, and still others numerical systems. Grades also varied in what they signified. Some educators believed that grades should reflect academic achievement alone, whereas others argued in favor of including other traditional measures like behavior. Half of high schools at the time still included a "deportment" category on report cards, and half of elementary schools included an "effort" category in their grading schemes.[33] Moreover, grades couldn't even be compared across classrooms, since each teacher had their own set of standards. As one commentator of the period noted: "the problem now presented is that of establishing a method whereby grades assigned by one teacher can be intelligently compared with those assigned by another, and all brought to a common standard."[34]

One upshot of this inability to compare across schools and communities was that discussions about school quality were often rooted not in evidence about what students were learning but, instead, in how often students were attending. The percentage of students who attended a district's schools each day was the closest proxy for school quality—a sign of whether educational infrastructure, funded at taxpayer expense, was being utilized efficiently.[35] Concerns about "overaged" children clogging up the lower grades of schools became a common concern of school officials and school reformers. These statistics could provide suggestive evidence of inefficient organization, poorly trained teachers, or subpar pedagogy, but they could not speak directly to what was going on inside of classrooms.[36] Though neither attendance records nor grades were suitable for this purpose, another technology presumably was: standardized assessments.

Each decade of the twentieth century had brought considerable growth in school enrollments and the average number of years a student spent in school. Many viewed these enrollment increases, especially at the high school level, as evidence that teachers were rewarding "mere attendance" and that schools had ceased to be institutions defined by rigorous competition and merit. If teachers were engaging in social promotion at the expense of maintaining educational standards, the result would be an undermining of the public's faith in schools. As one author in the 1920s explained, "Diplomas are hallmarks of excellence like the chemical manufacturer's 'C.P.' guaranty . . . [and must] be kept according to some uniform system intelligible to the people most vitally interested—the public."[37] Just as troubling, as educational achievement became more closely tied with individual advancement and labor market opportunities, a lack of uniformity in grading meant that some students might be undeservedly rewarded and others unfairly held back. As an observer at the University of Missouri wrote in 1911, "the grade has in more than one sense a cash value, and if there is no uniformity of grading in an institution, this means that the values are stolen from some and undeservedly presented to others."[38]

These concerns led some to argue that teacher-issued grades needed to be more like standardized tests. That is, that grades should distinguish between categories of pupils and that the distribution of grades, like so many natural phenomena, should follow a normal curve. "Native ability," wrote Isador Finkelstein in his treatise *The Marking System in Theory and Practice,* "behaves like any other biological trait." As such, "in any population its distribution is that known as the curve of error, the probability curve, or Gauss's curve."[39] School grades, he argued, should be devised accordingly, "based upon the orientation of all students around a central group whose accomplishment is construed to be average or medium."[40]

Though the influence of the mental testing movement, with its signature reliance upon IQ tests, fostered a belief that normal curves should be at the center of school-based evaluations, many educators worried about whether enshrining the normal curve in classrooms was really in the best interest of students. In response to studies that seemed to suggest that teachers could not reliably grade student work or produce a clear distribution of grades, one educator countered that "it is time for the science of education . . . to make [the normal curve] merely one of a class of teacher curves, all different and having function of significance. In fact, the usefulness of the teacher curve . . . has been scandalously overlooked."[41] Among the values espoused in allowing teachers to grade students in alternate ways was the inculcation of students' desire to learn for learning's sake, rather than in pursuit of grades. As Thorsten Veblen complained in 1918, the "system of academic grading and credit . . . resistlessly bends more and more of current instruction to its mechanical tests and progressively sterilizes all personal initiative and ambition that comes within its sweep."[42]

The idea that schools were putting their own organizational needs ahead of those of students was a particular concern among progressive educators. John Dewey and his many disciples worried that curricula were delivered at the expense of children's intrinsic interests and curiosities, an approach made worse by an emphasis on the accumulation of grades and credits. As one author wrote, "Following the influence of John Dewey, many educators have been trying to get activities in education to be motivated by intrinsic interest of the pupil. In this attempt they have attacked the giving of marks on the basis that the pupils tended to work because they desired high marks rather than because of their interest in the subject."[43] Another author of the period went even further, arguing that an emphasis on communicating student progress through grades was inherently incompatible with the intrinsic motivation of students, rcquiring a reevaluation of the entire practice of issuing and reporting grades. The report card, "which was once considered to be of almost divine origin, has been challenged to mortal combat." It was, as she noted, a "challenge from a group of young crusaders who have chosen to be known as the Intrinsic Clan against the entire family whose surname is Extrinsic."[44]

Though many educators continued to hold the line on the importance of intrinsic motivation in students, the inertia behind grading practices was too much to overcome. Attempts to replace grades and report cards with "diagnostic letters," for instance, were sporadically launched and quickly discarded. As one teacher at Westwood High School in Los Angeles noted, though "the suggestion of substituting a letter to the home in place of the formal mark was considered at some length," it was ultimately decided that even narrative letters would eventually "become as meaningless and as stereotyped as the subject marks they replaced."[45] Grades would need to be entirely eliminated if they were to avoid what opponents derided as "false standards of value among pupils." But eliminating grades was simply not feasible because, as V. L. Beggs noted in 1936, "A majority of parents, and too many teachers conclude that the school's most important contribution to the child's education is recorded on the card."[46]

Even beyond parental expectations, other schools in the increasingly national K-12 education system came to see grades as important inputs for their own work. As schools diversified their curricular offerings into distinct tracks—collegiate, vocational, and so on—administrators expected grades to create distinctions among students, which educators understood to be a hallmark of fairness and efficiency. A democratic system of schools, they argued, would ensure that everyone was educated according to his or her abilities and would not try to give everyone the same thing. In such a view, reliable grading systems were key features of efficient and well-organized schools. Moreover, they were crucial to the work of other institutions in the system. A report on college enrollments, for example, noted that many schools "which formerly admitted by examination" had moved to accept only "students who rank high in the secondary school"—a tendency "influenced by a number of studies which show a high relation between high-school rank and success in college."[47]

Thus, even as standardized testing became a prominent feature of American schooling, grades were still seen as an integral part of communicating with families about student academic progress and for tying larger numbers of institutions together into a national system of schools.

Creating a Permanent Record

When the public education system was first created there was no such thing as a transcript. It was only as schools began to generate information about student performance—attendance, grades, test scores—and as school achievement became associated with an individual's career prospects that it made sense for schools to record the information they created. As with the creation of grades and standardized tests, the creation of the permanent record was a function of the dual demands of communicating clearly to parents and educators, and of synchronizing the pieces of a disparate, non-uniform school system.

The earliest document that might be considered a student record was an annual "child census." These censuses were often required by states as they developed their early public school systems and were used for the purpose of assessing taxes, apportioning state funds, and, later, determining the denominator for school attendance rates. These were records of children who should be students, but they weren't *student* records—they didn't record individual attendance or achievement or progress. The need for individual records changed, however, once states passed compulsory school laws that required all children of a certain age to attend. Now schools within districts were increasingly expected to maintain common sets of records that allowed information to be transferred from school to school in order to keep track of students and verify that families were complying with school laws. In addition to being good for record-keeping, the practice was intended to thwart an excuse common among youth stopped by truant officers: they weren't absent, they were simply making their way across town to the school where they were enrolled or were seeking to transfer. A quick check of a school's records could determine the truth of the claim—and whether the student's family would be issued a warning, or a fine, or worse.[48]

Even when truant officers weren't involved, however, records needed to pass among schools. As American youth enrolled in more schooling, and as more students made it beyond the elementary grades, records of their attendance and school attainment had to be shared. These imperatives, initiated by a new generation of administrators intent on bringing order and efficiency to school systems, produced a bonanza of record-keeping. Ironically, these efforts aimed at order and standardization produced literally thousands of idiosyncratic styles. One 1925 study, for instance, found 1,515 different kinds of school records being kept, about half of which were unique to an individual school district.[49] Schools tracked student academic work, physical health, psychological evaluations, behavioral history, and more, but no standard form for doing so existed.

While these records were useful for serving the needs of local educators and their schools, they posed a serious challenge to the smooth administration of the public education system. As with the push to introduce standardized tests of student learning, school reformers seeking to build an education system, and not just a series of isolated institutions, realized that some uniformity and synchronization was necessary across schools. This is because records only work if institutions that issue and receive them can make sense of them and use them to accomplish necessary tasks; otherwise, what has been recorded is just random bits of information. In order for administrators to compare the relative performance of their schools, and in order to allow students to continue on their educational journeys, even as they moved between schools, some set of agreed upon information would need to be recorded and shared.

Those at the forefront of the effort to standardize record-keeping, people like Columbia University professors George Strayer and Nickolaus Engelhardt, viewed their efforts explicitly in terms of solidifying relationships among schools through the sharing of common information. As they put it, "A system of records and reports which will cement an entire state and even the nation in its educational undertakings . . . has been recognized as one of the greatest needs."[50] The idea that schools would need to create records in order to "cement . . . the nation in its educational undertakings" might seem hard to grasp. That's because a student currently enrolling in elementary school faces no uncertainty about his or her path through our multilevel education system: what starts in elementary school continues in middle and high school and, for many students, culminates in a two- or four-year postsecondary institution. But this path of attainment and advancement was not always so clear.

For most of the early history of American schooling, there was no clear delineation between the upper levels of the school system. At the time, most high schools and colleges were more interested in increasing enrollments (and the tuition dollars that came with them) than in maintaining high admissions standards. In practice, this meant that many colleges had large "preparatory departments" that sought to prepare students for college level work. This allowed colleges to enroll students, and collect tuition money, even before those students were ready for college-level work.

This practice came to an end, however, as a result of the intervention of the Carnegie Foundation for the Advancement of Teaching in the first decades of the twentieth century. The foundation, which sought to create a pension plan for teachers and professors (still around today as TIAA-CREF), created important stipulations for institutions that wanted to participate. The foundation sought to break the cycle of competition that often encouraged colleges to lower standards in order to attract students. Their aim was to create a clear demarcation between colleges and high schools: an institution would not be recognized as a college if it accepted students with fewer than fourteen units of prior academic preparation. The idea was that if an institution was willing to enroll students with less preparation, there was a decent chance the institution was still operating as a preparatory department and not as a proper college or university.[51]

Accepting the formal constraints placed on them by the Carnegie Foundation was mutually beneficial to high schools and colleges because it gave them each a distinct market for students. Now, students who wanted to reach the highest levels of the school system would have to pass through both institutions, one after the other. Agreeing to share the educational careers of students also meant agreeing to standardize the way they measured and communicated about student progress. The result called for a common system of academic currency that would allow students to exchange their high school courses for admission into higher education. Though some universities and, later, regional accreditation bodies sought to avoid this record-keeping step by accrediting high schools directly—declaring any graduate of the high school automatically eligible for admission—the expansion of the curriculum and the number of high schools and students made this increasingly difficult. The currency developed to mark student progress, the Carnegie unit, became the coin of the realm, and the transcript became the student's balance sheet.[52]

Once schools had established the practice of individualized record-keeping and adopted a common unit of recording academic progress, it was easy for these records—sparse though they were—to accommodate other information like grades and test scores.

"Earmarks of an up-to-Date School System"

By the end of the Progressive Era, American schools had developed and integrated two forms of assessment—teacher-issued grades and normed standardized tests—as well as a way to faithfully record and preserve them both for future inspection. Crucially, though these forms of assessment might appear on the same transcript, they continued to serve distinct but overlapping purposes. Despite complaints that teacher grades were subjective, unreliable, and generally did not conform to the properties of a normal distribution, grades remained an important form of communication between teachers and students, and an important record of student attainment that could be shared with parents and future schools. Standardized tests could also serve to communicate about student performance and to make distinctions among groups of students; but because of the decentralized character of American schools, these standardized tests necessarily operated at a distance from individual classrooms. Over the next two decades, the development of grading and testing practices would be characterized by more clearly delineating the role each would play in the operation of the American school system. While grades would remain important local dialects, the shift away from local control and toward state and federal governance meant that schools would increasingly rely on standardized test scores as the system's lingua franca.

These developments would not have been possible if not for the massive growth of the standardized testing industry in the 1920s. The value of large-scale standardized testing for assessing and sorting people was on full display during World War I. The results of standardized tests became an important component of the military's bureaucratic machinery for fitting people into the "right jobs"—a capacity the military would expand on substantially in World War II with more and more elaborate assessments devised to increase the efficiency of military training.

The upshot of this investment in standardized assessments was a cadre of professionals newly trained to use standardized tests in bureaucratic settings. When the war was over, these experts migrated to other large organizations that were interested in their expertise— namely, large businesses and school districts. As US commissioner of education Philandor Claxton remarked, "the fact that two or three hundred young men who have for several months been working in the psychology division of the Army are now about to be discharged offers an unusual opportunity for city schools to obtain the services of competent men as directors of departments of psychology and efficiency, for such purposes as measuring the results of teaching and establishing standards to be attained in the several school studies."[53]

Not surprisingly, having a well-elaborated testing system became a mark of a modern, sophisticated organization. As one author wrote in 1921, "measurement work is now generally regarded in leading educational circles as one of the earmarks of an up-to-date school system," and brought with it a certain "prestige value." Teachers and communities, he noted, may be somewhat skeptical of the work. But they could be won over, he argued, by the suggestion "that those opposing measurement work are thereby in danger of being considered unprogressive."[54]

The explosive growth of the standardized testing industry made it relatively easy for schools to pick and choose from among the available tests. With more than 300 tests available to American educators, it was possible, for instance, to use IQ tests for the general assessment of students' "innate" abilities, the Stanford Achievement Test or Iowa Test of Basic Skills to ascertain students' general academic attainment relative to national norms, and the Kansas Silent Reading test to assess students in development of this particularly important skill.

Because this was a commercial enterprise, test developers went to great lengths to make tests easy to administer, grade, and interpret. Describing his design philosophy, the creator of the Kansas Silent Reading test explained, "it should be so simple in its arrangement and in the plan for giving it and scoring the results derived from it that a teacher unskilled in the use of standard tests can understand without difficulty what is expected of her in giving and scoring the test . . . the time consumed in giving the test and in doing the necessary work for scoring should not be so great as to make teachers who do the work feel that it is a task out of proportion to the good derived from doing it."[55]

Ironically, one result of the pervasive use of a wide array of standardized tests in K-12 schools was the accommodation of local variation. Standardized tests provided a uniform superstructure that could be dropped down onto existing systems. This dynamic was particularly evident in the development of two of the most important tests of the twentieth century: the SAT and the GED. While many colleges and universities had traditionally relied on either individualized entrance examinations or the pre-certification of individual high schools—a process by which graduates of particular schools were automatically eligible for admission—such approaches proved unwieldy as the geographic scope of student recruitment grew. With no standardized courses of study, no universal curricula, and no uniform system of grading, it became increasingly difficult for colleges to determine the most qualified applicants.

In typical American fashion, the response to this lack of uniformity was not a national conference to set a standard criterion for issuing a high school diploma, but independent action by a small subset of elite schools. These schools came together to create an independent membership organization that would create a standardized examination for use in their admissions process. The result was the creation of the SAT.[56] The SAT was valuable precisely because it could provide a uniform measure of comparison of students without reference to any individual student's high school course taking.

Though the context was different, the same agnostic stance on local standards was the decisive feature in the adoption and long-term utility of the GED. The General Educational Development test was developed during World War II as a way of certifying the

schooling equivalency of the more than half of US veterans who had
not graduated from high school. The lack of uniform high school
standards, within and across states, meant that the test developers
necessarily had to fall back on broad categories of learning and generic skills that reflected no particular pedagogy or curriculum, lest
a veteran from a particular state be placed at a disadvantage.[57]

The effort to secure recognition for the GED's high school
equivalency standard was aided by sympathy toward returning GIs
and by the involvement of some of the nation's most famous testing
experts, notably Ralph Tyler and E. F. Lindquist. But the fact that
the GED would achieve near universal adoption within two years
of its introduction, despite the total lack of curricular uniformity
across states, indicates how comfortable American educators were
in moving between the universal realm of standardized tests and the
particular contexts of their own schools. It is not surprising, then,
that although the GED was intended to be a temporary program
for World War II veterans, it was soon authorized for use with
all adults over school age and, eventually, for students as young as
sixteen.

The tendency to accommodate local variation by overlaying a
national standardized test extended not just to individual assessments
like the GED and SAT, but also to assessments intended to inform
the public about schooling. In the 1960s, as education increasingly
came to be seen as a front in the Cold War, the federal government
took an increasing interest in developing ways to inform itself and
the public about educational outcomes. Fear that the federal government might use these tools to inappropriately monitor or exert
influence over individual state or district schools or, worse yet, try
to become a national school board and advance a national agenda,
resulted in assessments that purported to speak in generalized terms

about the "American student" or the "American high school," despite there being no such thing in practice.

The most notable example of this was the design and creation of the National Assessment of Educational Progress (NAEP). In a sign of how new this way of thinking at a national level about student achievement was, the first iterations of NAEP avoided making any singular pronouncement about how American students were doing in school. Instead, NAEP published each test item individually along with the percentage of students at each age level who got the item correct. As the public became more comfortable with this new, more abstract way of thinking about the national performance of fundamentally locally and state-directed schools, subsequent iterations of NAEP attached a specific score to the performance of nine-, twelve-, and seventeen-year-olds, making it possible to track the general performance of American students over time.

Despite the lack of actionable information provided by these scores (a concerned citizen or policymaker can only guess what fluctuations in reported scores mean for their state or local schools), these scores have become a perennial part of discussions about US schools. Indeed, each decade has brought calls for the production of more, and more disaggregated, NAEP results.[58] Despite the persistent and considerable variation in standards, curriculum, and teacher licensure requirements, NAEP has made it possible to compare the performance of students across all states and large urban districts—a task dutifully performed by the media with each new release of results.[59]

The widespread adoption of national assessments like the GED, the SAT and ACT, and NAEP did not supplant state and local discussions about standards or the use of grades. Instead, they created a system with robust alternatives and multiple ways of communicating similar information. The consequences of these developments are not easily characterized as either good or bad, but they clearly illuminate the crosscutting interests of our current approaches to evaluation. The existence of the SAT provides a means for colleges and universities to independently compare the performance of two students with otherwise different schooling experiences, obviating the need for a uniform curriculum. But in order to make that comparison in even a nominally fair way, the SAT must require that students engage in a high-stakes assessment that bears only a passing resemblance to the day-to-day work of schools. The same is true for citizens trying to derive the quality of local schools from state and national assessments. The assessments provide some basis for comparison, but one that is necessarily abstract and disassociated from specific elements like textbooks or pedagogy. The persistence of grades offers a more direct measure of students' work and a check on the influence of the SAT; but because grades are not standardized and schools vary in their level of rigor, it can create incentives for students to do enough to "get an A," even if it comes at the expense of deeper engagement and learning.

Coming to Grips with Assessment

Though there is nothing inevitable about the system of grades, test scores, and transcripts currently in use throughout US schools, there is nothing arbitrary about them either. As this brief examination of the history of assessment technologies has hopefully illustrated, generations of Americans and American educators saw the practices that we now take for granted today as crucial interventions in a system that was perceived as failing to meet the crosscutting needs of its many stakeholders.

Yet the quantification of student learning has come at a steep cost—a cost that we are often oblivious to, given how pervasive grading, rating, and ranking is in our schools. From elementary school through graduate programs, student learning is consistently distorted and devalued in ways that are both pervasive and inequitable. It might seem that we have to choose between keeping something that is deeply flawed or jettisoning something that serves a functional purpose. But we think this kind of framing is a trap—a trap that can be avoided by carefully delineating the specific uses our technologies were developed to perform and, just as importantly, understanding how these uses were defined by and integrated into the operation of the education system as a whole. This means considering each technology individually, and as a part of a larger package of assessment tools. It also means, as we argued in Chapters 1–3, that these technologies and their functions remain the subject of considerable interest and concern among students, parents, teachers, and the general public.

The key to reform, then, is not to reinvent the system, but to recalibrate it. This task requires that we account for the historical development not only of how these tools became embedded in our school system, but also of how they became embedded in our cultural expectations about what schools do—the subject of our next chapter.

5

The Culture of Assessment

"Tests are just a part of life. You can't avoid tests." So said Congressman Michael Capuano in a 2014 speech that was otherwise highly critical of testing.[1] A letter from an independent Bay Area school sent home to parents intending to prepare families for a week of testing makes much the same point: "Although the relationship between [the standardized assessment] and our curriculum is at times imperfect, we recognize that standardized tests are also a part of life, and we want to prepare our students for this reality."[2] The congressman's point, like that in the newsletter, is the same: we may not like assessment, but we have to live with it.

This attitude is common among Americans. They grumble about grades and lament the ubiquity of testing. They often view transcripts as traps from which there is no escape—think of the terror inspired by the phrase "this will go down in your permanent record." But they generally operate as if assessment is an inescapable feature of the natural world. And that's a major stumbling block for any would-be reformer seeking to change the way we measure student learning.

So, if assessment is so problematic—a theme of the first three chapters of this book—why do Americans put up with it? As we suggest in this chapter, there are three reasons for this remarkable endurance.

The first reason is exposure. Grades, tests, and transcripts are a part of what Mary Metz once called "real school," and what David Tyack and Larry Cuban called the "grammar of schooling."[3] Assessment, in other words, is a feature without which a school wouldn't be considered legitimate. Imagine a school with no grades, no standardized tests, and no transcripts. Though some of us might like the sound of such an assessment-free environment, others simply wouldn't accept it. Indeed, the fact that a small number of schools market themselves around such exceptionalism helps prove the general rule about our expectations around grades, ratings, and rankings.

The second factor explaining the endurance of grades, tests, and transcripts is bureaucracy. At every level of the American education system, information about students and schools is created, shared, and stored. That isn't by accident. The system requires the flow of information to synchronize itself—to ensure that students at one level of the system are ready to move on to the next level, or to preserve a student's academic record for use sometime in the future. In a face-to-face society, such information could be conveyed via observation or conversation. Yet the sheer volume of students and schools in the United States—roughly fifty million young people dispersed across nearly a hundred thousand schools in public K-12 education alone, to say nothing of private K-12 schools or higher education—makes firsthand experience impossible. As a result, schools, employers, and the state have come to rely on the compression of information through letters, numbers, and ledgers. The system, in other words, depends on assessment results. No wonder that data collection has expanded to the degree that it has, raising alarm bells among privacy advocates.

The third reason is that despite our penchant for complaining about assessment, most of us find it useful. Beyond seeing it as inescapable, students and their families engage with grades, ratings, and rankings to gain access to colleges, jobs, and even discount insurance rates. The right kind of academic record has made students eligible for a wide range of opportunities—from school sports to military deferment. Inasmuch as that is the case, Americans tend to view their assessment results as important for school and beyond. In fact, many view them as indicators of their ability or achievement, making them less inclined to resist the process of assessment. The sheer variety of assessments also means that people, whether individual students or boosters for a local district, can pick among the variety of available data points to make their case for why they deserve recognition. As long as the system produces winners, there will be opposition to unmaking it.

The Grammar of Assessment

Schooling is a fundamentally conservative enterprise. That is, despite the day-to-day angst about our schools, they tend to change incrementally and mostly in small ways over time. The main reason for this is that stakeholders, themselves, tend to resist radical reform of their schools.

In a country that enthusiastically embraces the notion of innovation, that may seem surprising. But education is a special field in that nearly all adults have experienced the system firsthand. Before they become teachers, principals, or parents of school-aged children, Americans spend roughly a dozen years in the schools. They aren't brainwashed or indoctrinated there. Yet that lengthy exposure does establish a very deep-seated sense of what a "normal school" looks like, how it operates, and what kind of things go on there.

Consider how this impacts teachers. As scholars of education have documented, teachers tend to teach as they were taught.[4] That is, the "instructional core" of classrooms—scholar Dick Elmore's phrase for the interaction between teachers and students around curriculum—has remained markedly stable. Why?

Before teachers receive any formal professional preparation, they experience a long period of informal training—what sociologist Dan Lortie called "the apprenticeship of observation."[5] Because all teachers in the United States must possess college degrees, we know that all new educators have gone through at least seventeen years of schooling. Watching teachers for nearly two decades, they become acculturated to particular norms. Not only do future teachers observe these norms while in school, but they also tend to be drawn disproportionately from the pool of students who thrived in school; in other words, those norms served them well. Thus, when it comes time to teach, educators tend to draw on the practices of their predecessors, further embedding those techniques and procedures as classroom norms.

Certainly, there are students who don't like being graded, and who find grades demotivating. There are students who perceive standardized tests as a waste of time. And without question there are students who would like to do away with every possible version of the permanent record. Yet, those with sharply divergent ideas about grading, rating, and ranking are often convinced through their experiences that school isn't for them, or at least that *teaching* isn't for them. By contrast, those who experience positive reinforcement—those for whom school feels pleasurable and rewarding—are much more likely to seek out education as a career.[6]

It is important here to recognize that teachers are not unthinking automatons. Many educators see the downside of grading, are opposed to the problematic use of standardized testing, and are aware of the negative impact that a permanent record can have on students. But these views are much more likely to play out in small ways, rather than in fundamental changes to the system. And alternative assessment practices are likely to be hemmed in by a certain school culture around assessment.

Equally important in determining the conventional tendencies of schools are parents and families. Having themselves once crammed for final exams, drilled on vocabulary flashcards for the SAT, or toiled away to raise their grade point averages, many parents are inclined to view assessment as an important feature of the education system. What kind of school doesn't give grades? What do you mean there are no tests? How will my kid get into college if there are no transcripts?

There are countless examples of well-meaning and potentially valuable reform efforts that have run aground on suddenly visible, rock-solid beliefs about how schools should operate. Consider the backlash that often ensues whenever a district opts for a new math curriculum: a parent checks in on his or her child struggling to complete the assigned math homework, only to find that it's impossible to make heads or tails of what the teacher wants. The parent definitely knows how to subtract three-digit numbers, just not like *this.* "What on earth," the parent wonders (and posts on social media), "is going on in the schools?"[7] Of course, sometimes parental responses to curricular changes are because a school subject has become a symbol in a larger culture war—whether about evolution, sex education, or critical race theory.[8] But that need not be the only source of concern. Changes that sever the tie between parents' school experiences and those of their children feel threatening—an affront to their own time in school and their demonstrated abilities.

Parental responses to changes that involve assessment, rather than just curricular changes, can be particularly intense. Consider what happened in many districts across the country when, in the midst of a once-in-a-century pandemic, schools moved to cancel grades for the semester or opt everyone into a pass / fail option. The result was a fierce outcry from parents, thousands of whom went online and signed a petition created by a group calling themselves "HS Grading Equity for All." Here it is worth quoting the petition at length, as it captures the level of anxiety that attends even temporary changes in assessment practices and how deeply intertwined and far-reaching the stakes are perceived to be:

> Without a letter grade for this semester, all high school students will be unable to raise their GPA and thus be at a disadvantage when competing for scholarships, college entrance placement and merit aid. This especially affects those juniors who will apply in the fall for college. As it currently stands with Pass / Incomplete, the GPAs that they apply to colleges with will be from January 2020, and since students now do not have the opportunity to meet their goals for their GPA, they may be adversely affected when being considered for scholarship opportunities and competitive college acceptances. In the current economy, with so much job loss, these extra merit dollars can make a difference regarding whether students can afford

college tuition. Even more problematic for the class of 2021, many colleges are no longer requiring SAT or ACT scores, thus making GPAs matter more during college acceptance process. Additionally, missing an entire semesters worth of GPA puts all Oregon students at a disadvantage when competing against students from other states with a full high school career of letter grades . . . [Oregon Department of Education] says they are instituting this policy in the interest of equity. However, this decision provides no equity or fairness for students who have worked hard to earn their grades.[9]

To summarize, these parents were concerned that the conversion of one semester of grades to pass / fail would result in (1) depriving students an opportunity to improve their GPAs; (2) harming students' opportunities to (a) get accepted into college, (b) earn a scholarship, and (c) afford college tuition; in part by (3) making students less competitive against, or less comparable to, students from other states; and, because colleges have made other changes to the traditional assessment system by dropping the SAT, (4) undermining students' GPAs at the moment they are more important than ever.

If all that wasn't enough, there is the issue of "fairness." To have a student work hard in high school and not have a good grade to show for his or her efforts undermines any claim to fairness in the proposed policy, or so the logic goes. In the parents' view, the schools are reneging on a long-standing contract: hard work at school is rewarded with good grades.

There is another dynamic at play here, which concerns not just the objections of parents, but also the matter over which parents are most likely to object. Although roughly 60 percent of American students will attend some form of higher education, only a small percentage will attend selective four-year institutions.[10] And yet, this vocal minority of parents is most likely to object to changes in grading, because they have the most invested in educational assessments and the rewards they are likely to offer. The voices of these parents are often backed by those who didn't personally succeed in school—either because they were not given the chance, or because they weren't well served by their schools—who believe that academic success is critical for their own children's upward mobility.[11]

This is true not just in exceptional cases like a pandemic, but also in response to policy changes made under traditional circumstances. For instance, a statewide effort to move from traditional grades to proficiency-based evaluations resulting in 0–4 scores for each evaluated outcome met with strong resistance from parents in Maine. Among their objections: concern that the shift would prevent the calculation of traditional GPAs or the identification of valedictorians.[12] Likewise, efforts to eliminate honors tracks or the number of AP courses that students can take in a given semester are frequently met with hostility and pushback on the grounds that they disadvantage students relative to their peers in other schools. With stakes this high, unilateral disarmament feels like an extremely risky strategy. Better to stay the course.

Once the terms of assessment have been set, an elaborate choreography emerges around what "normal" school practices are. Many teachers develop, and sometimes actively cultivate, reputations rooted strictly in what kind of "grader" they are. Tough graders, though sometimes hated by their students, are often viewed with respect and esteem. Classes known for being "easy As," by contrast, are viewed as something close to a waste of time. In each of these cases, the process of grading is viewed as a proxy for rigor.

Consideration of how difficult it will be to earn one's desired grade is a reasonable and predictable basis for selecting courses. Rate

My Professors—a website where college students can post unmoderated reviews of instructors and courses—asks students to provide a "difficulty" rating for each professor, which is clearly understood by those who post on the site to mean "how hard was it to get an A?" In a more formal context, when Cornell began posting information about grade distributions for each course online—ostensibly to help better contextualize for students the meaning of grades—researchers found that students used that information to select more leniently graded courses. The result, perhaps not surprisingly, was increased grade inflation.[13] An experiment conducted at Stanford, using an online course information tool, found that students were particularly interested in accessing information about historical grade distributions. One key factor that they were interested in: how many hours prior students spent each week on work for the course.[14]

The Structure of Assessment

Approaches to assessment aren't just sustained by culture. They are supported by a series of structures that nudges people in particular directions. Consider the teacher gradebook. Though such products differ, the core element in the gradebook is essentially a spreadsheet with spaces for student names, the titles of key assessments, and scores. Each "score box" is large enough for either a grade (A–F) or a number (1–100); no narrative description would ever fit. It ends with a sum total that aggregates all student work into a single figure.

Online tools like PowerSchool and Blackboard are the same. There is space for narrative comments, but the system runs on scores, which compile into final grades. The increasingly common practice of giving parents access to these spaces, so that they can track their children's assignments and monitor more directly how their children are doing in a class, only serves to reinforce the idea that what school is fundamentally about is the turning in and grading of assignments.

The gradebook is a tool in service of the "grading period." Between two and six times each year, K-12 educators and postsecondary instructors are required to enter grades for students. Often these grades are in service of larger reporting or early alert systems. Many middle and high schools, for instance, require that students receive a midterm progress report—one that often has to be formally acknowledged by parents. Many colleges and universities require that professors do the same, specifically for the college athletes in the class—so coaches and athletes have a heads-up about who might be trending toward academic ineligibility.

To be clear, timely communication about school performance is important and systems that facilitate this can be valuable, especially if the alternative is that there is no communication at all. But these systems come with trade-offs. Undoubtedly, there are some instructors who ignore the demands of these reporting systems and structure their courses, assignment due dates, and the delivery of grades and feedback based on the rhythms of the course rather than the imperative to generate data. But in our experience, most instructors feel the pull of these requirements—the need to have *something* to enter in the gradebook.

In addition to the pull of the gradebook, a range of resources encourages a particular approach to assessment. Some instructors, certainly, generate their own projects or activities. But textbooks generally offer their own set of assessment tools, which most often take the form of tests. The "teacher's edition" of most textbooks come with tests (and answers!) conveniently placed at the back of the book. There are quizzes and unit tests and final exams that are all bundled together.

Digital resources also encourage traditional assessment practices. Many, for instance, will automatically grade student tests if an instructor uses a format like multiple choice and enters an "answer key." Developments in online instruction and course delivery have only amplified this basic structure. Instructors are frequently given the advice to embed quizzes into their video lectures every few minutes to check for student understanding. The results of some of these quizzes are treated as ephemeral, but for many instructors this "engagement" is treated as an evaluation and duly recorded in the gradebook.

So far, we have considered only the assignments and tests that the teacher develops or uses to mark progress in the course. There is, of course, the larger structure of standardized tests that are required and that assert themselves on the structure and rhythms of the course. The curriculum and pace of virtually every AP class in the country is dictated by the date of the annual AP examination. Even putting these specialized, advanced courses aside, virtually every teacher can tell you when their school's annual state-mandated testing period is—the days or weeks in which high-stakes standardized tests are issued in K-12 schools. Even if teachers do not teach in one of the tested subjects, most know better than to schedule projects or exams during the testing period. Some schools and districts go so far as to take the issue out of teachers' hands by having a specific schedule for standardized testing days.

Many people mistakenly believe that the majority of these standardized tests are the exclusive result of federal mandates stemming from No Child Left Behind (NCLB) or its successor legislation, the Every Student Succeeds Act (ESSA). But this is a misconception, which shows how deeply embedded standardized testing is across every level of the system. A detailed study of the standardized testing schedules in fourteen urban and rural districts, for instance, found that district assessments are more numerous and more time-consuming than the state assessments required by federal law. The study also found that students take district- or state-mandated standardized tests once a month on average, and as often as twice a month, and that's before taking into account the test preparation activities that regularly surround these testing events.[15] This is quite a message to send to students about what schooling is all about. It's no wonder, then, that students consider standardized testing to be synonymous with the school experience.

Testing has become such a foundational part of assessment that it has become the default way for politicians to signal the importance of a skill, subject, or transition. The selection of math and English language arts (and the omission of, say, art) for mandatory annual testing under federal law was not accidental. It was an intentional signal, to both schools and the public, that these were the foundational academic subjects. In the 1970s, politicians sought to assuage public fears about declining standards and a lack of attention to basic skills by requiring students to pass "exit examinations" in order to receive their high school diplomas. The fact that there is no evidence that such examinations improve academic outcomes, or that they raise academic standards, is beside the point. The point was that imposing a testing requirement was a way of communicating the seriousness of the issue and the robustness of the response.

Even beyond the standardized tests that give shape to students' week-to-week schooling experiences, there are the tests that serve as gatekeepers to higher levels of attainment. There is perhaps no better example of this than the introduction of the GED, which, when it was first introduced in the 1940s, required a passing score barely above the level of random guessing. Creating a test that everyone can pass but requiring that they take it anyway in order to earn their diploma and move on to postsecondary education is a strong indicator of how much Americans *culturally* believe that tests should mark the transitions in our school life.[16]

Though set at a much higher degree of difficulty, there are also the other standardized tests that are built into the college application process. Even though many four-year colleges and universities no longer require the SAT and ACT for admission, a majority still do. And many of them also award an advantage in the admissions process to students who have impressive AP exam scores. Even students who go to college and find a relative reprieve from standardized testing will find that they have still more gatekeeping tests in their future, whether it is the GMAT for business school, the MCAT for medical school, the LSAT for law school, or the GRE for virtually every other graduate school program one could imagine applying to. The message of the system is clear: educational advancement is inseparable from standardized testing.

Fuel for Bureaucracies

Just as there is a popular culture of assessment—a set of norms guiding the way we measure student learning—there is also a bureaucratic culture of assessment. Various offices and agencies consider the production of test score information a core feature of their work, and still others have developed standard operating procedures predicated on the availability of metrics like grade point averages or standardized test scores. Many of these bureaucratic systems simply could not function without the letters and numbers that reduce learning to something compatible with a spreadsheet.

The quantitative analytic revolution of the 1960s was a major watershed moment in development of the bureaucratic infrastructure that fosters the culture of assessment. Spurred by the increasing ambition of the federal government to direct education policy, and enabled by advances in computing power, the production of test scores was seen as necessary to monitor and evaluate schools. Whether it was the Coleman Report, NAEP, or evaluation of federally funded educational programs, test scores became the foundational "objective measure" of educational achievement. Indeed, when Congress passed the Elementary and Secondary Education Act in 1965, it included for the first time a requirement that programs funded under Title I of the law conduct evaluations that included "objective measurement of educational achievement"—in other words, test scores.

The evaluation requirements of Title I programs may seem relatively minor compared to the huge investments of resources and time necessary to fulfill the annual testing requirements of NCLB or ESSA, but the overall effect is the same: orienting work around the production, dissemination, and analysis of test scores. Moreover, once the scores are available, they become the primary way of "seeing" and communicating about schools. When state or federal officials want to talk about how schools are doing, or when they want to craft a narrative of progress or decline, they almost always do so with reference to test scores. More often than not, these narratives end up being echoed across news media, further tying the broader public discussion to test scores.[17]

Assessment inputs don't just influence our narratives; they also serve as critical infrastructure for synchronizing our school system.

The American education system isn't uniform by any stretch of the imagination; and to the extent that it is a system at all, it might best be described as a "Rube Goldberg state" held together by inefficient and often unexpected workarounds.[18] Over three million teachers are spread across roughly thirteen thousand districts and nearly one hundred thousand public schools, collectively educating more than fifty million students. Add to that figure thirty-five thousand private schools serving just under five million students, as well as thousands of two-year and four-year colleges and universities. Though we may talk about an American education system, it is crucial to stress that it was not built as such. Instead, it was welded together in fits and starts over time, often simply by laying new elements onto the existing system.

Developing common units of measure, as we noted in Chapter 3, was key to the integration and synchronization of this system because it reduced the amount of administrative friction in daily operation. Bureaucracies run on succinct bits of information, which are organized by categorical rules rather than by individual judgment.[19] By setting a numerical cutoff or threshold, state employees don't have to make individual decisions based on their own personal judgment; instead, the system can run "mechanically," relying on the outputs of grades, ratings, and rankings. The upshot of this arrangement is that in order to keep the system running smoothly, we must continue to supply it with the necessary pieces of information, be they placement test scores, grade point averages, or official transcripts containing the right course title prerequisites to enroll in the next class.

While this emphasis on discrete, distilled bits of information might not seem ideal, there are reasons our system has evolved to sustain this kind of culture of assessment. Americans broadly believe that leaders have a responsibility for ensuring that schools are adequately serving students and responsibly managing taxpayer dollars. Doing so across a vast number of schools, and in a uniform and impartial way, requires moving away from individual interpretations and impressions and toward more uniform and ostensibly objective accounting measures.

No wonder, then, that despite the obvious limitations of standardized tests, accountability systems run on the currency of scores. Even if accountability systems weren't so narrowly designed, they would still require ledgers rather than anecdotes; that's how bureaucracies work. We can't simply take each principal's word. And it isn't feasible to ask each school to write a hundred-page report. Even if it were, who would read all of them? What, then, is the alternative to a system based on data? While there are other ways to gather information and render decisions, none of them are quite as simple.

Given the scale at which it operates and the requirements it faces with regard to transparency and record-keeping, the state needs information that is compressed and standardized. It requires something that is universally applicable, easily stored, and readily understood by anyone. In short, the system needs numbers for a ledger. That's why modern governments are so seemingly obsessed with "data"—because quantitative pictures of the world allow government to "see."[20]

This obsession perpetuates the bureaucratic culture of assessment. It also perpetuates the steady proliferation of new measures. The same features that make numbers such good inputs for bureaucratic procedures—they are stable, combinable, and easily shared—also allow them to be easily repurposed for new ends.[21] For instance, a student's single year test score combined with her scores from prior years can easily be used to calculate not just the student's level of proficiency but her rate of growth as well. And that information, combined with still more information about other students' rates of growth, can be used to calculate the performance of that class's *teacher*—a so-called value-added score.

The production of indicators based on second order calculations like this make the entire system further dependent on the continual production of scores. A single-year disruption to testing, then, means not only the loss of those scores but also the short-circuiting of teacher value-added measures and student growth calculations. To the degree that those ratings have been integrated into systems for the granting of tenure or of merit bonuses for teachers, or re-authorization decisions for charter schools, the downstream consequences can be significant and, thus, the incentive to avoid these disruptions even more so.

In short, though all bureaucratic systems tend to have a preference for succinct, numerical information that allows for rule-based decision-making, our education system has become especially reliant on these measures. They are what hold an otherwise vast and eclectic set of organizations together into a mostly functioning whole. The information is not only "useful," in that sense, but also self-perpetuating: it becomes the language of those working within the bureaucracy and, in turn, the language of the public. As a building block of the bureaucratic system, and the basis of public discourse, scores are embedded more deeply with each new elaboration of the system.

The negative implications of this approach are obvious. Test scores are hardly an accurate measure of school quality, and the unintended consequences of overreliance on them are well documented.[22] But the scores, themselves, aren't the problem. Instead, the problem is the narrowness of what counts as "data," coupled with the complete absence of human judgment in many of our assessment and accountability systems.[23] And the explanation for that is fairly simple: the ease with which bureaucratic systems can be erected to run on the language of numbers. Training people, paying them, and assigning them to visit schools and understand their quality—that's a major and ongoing task. Building quantification systems and pushing the "run" button? That's easy.

Getting Ahead: Assessment and Mobility

Much assessment isn't designed for a teacher's gradebook or a state's data system. The SAT and ACT tests, for instance, are assessment structures that normalize testing for all young people considering a four-year college pathway. The Advanced Placement program, similarly, culminates in an exam score that is reported to a student's future college or university. But it isn't just the college-bound who take extracurricular exams. Aspiring hairdressers, plumbers, electricians, doctors, and lawyers all have to take licensure tests. This makes sense given the state's general commitment to standardized testing and the public's broad acceptance of it.

The people most likely to resist assessment are those badly served by it. Students dogged by bad grades, aspiring professionals who fail their licensure exams, young people denied entrance to their preferred colleges—they all have reason to question the use of grades, tests, and transcripts. But they often lack the power and status of their higher-scoring peers. Someone who flunks out of college, for instance, is less likely to become the chancellor of the University of California system or the US secretary of education, and therefore less likely to bring about a major change.

By contrast, the "winners" of the system often have reason to think that assessment technologies work just fine. Grading, rating, and ranking, after all, identified *them* as deserving of whatever privileges or benefits they ended up with. And most of their peers in positions of influence have similar records—they earned good grades, they scored well on tests, they put together impressive transcripts, and they graduated from elite schools.

All of this, of course, is bound up in the idea that education is the surest way to get ahead in the United States. And that idea is rooted in a few simple beliefs. One of those beliefs is that status shouldn't be inherited—such things were ostensibly left behind in the Old World. A second belief is that talent rises to the top—America is a land of opportunity. A third belief is that the playing field in education is relatively equal—students are lined up together when the starting pistol is fired. Combined, these beliefs incline Americans to think that schools are an appropriate sorting ground for status competition. Take young people from various walks of life, throw open the doors to education, and let those who have demonstrated the most talent and ability use their natural advantages to win social and economic rewards.

Even in the early days of the republic, school was presented as a "great equalizer."[24] The founders, for instance, frequently referred to themselves as "Men of Merit," and Americans of that generation constructed a popular mythology about "self-made men" and an "aristocracy of talent."[25] Of course, it took nearly a century to build a system of public schools that would serve all white school-age children, and it took until the mid-twentieth century to expand access to racially minoritized populations, so we should be highly skeptical of such claims. But the key point here is that cultural ideas about "merit" have been around for centuries. And as schooling has become increasingly universal, it has become the key arena for meritocratic competition.

In a smaller, face-to-face society, the merits of individuals would be known through firsthand experience. Whether this was displayed in schools or outside of them, talent and ability would be apparent to observers. In a larger society, however, merit needs to be displayed *symbolically*—through compressed information that can be carried across time and space. Grades, tests, and transcripts have proved extremely useful in this manner. That isn't to say that any of these mechanisms for quantifying student learning fairly or accurately reflects student merit. But they do serve as a kind of national (and sometimes international) currency that can be exchanged for advantage.

Knowing all this, parents angle to secure every educational advantage for their children. And as they do, they approach schooling as a zero-sum game. After all, if *learning* is the aim, then everyone can win. But if the purpose of school is to get ahead, then somebody has to fail.[26] Thus it is that middle-class and affluent families engage in the practice of so-called opportunity hoarding—a means of class preservation driven by exclusionary behaviors like support for academic tracking or resistance to school integration.[27] There are a few major problems with this state of affairs, and they are worth detailing separately.

The first, and perhaps most obvious, is that the game is rigged. Students don't enter school on a level playing field. From the time their children are born, privileged families work to give their offspring an advantage—helping them develop prized skills, securing access to particular resources, and gaining entry into high-status institutions. Their conscious aim is to help their kids get ahead.

But even if parents didn't intentionally play an active role in exacerbating inequality, the fact is that broader social and economic inequality ensure that students enter school with vastly different levels of preparation. As a result, we see a second problem, which has been described as the "Matthew effect" ("the rich get richer and the poor get poorer").[28] Those who immediately begin succeeding in school are praised, develop positive school-oriented identities, and are placed in accelerated coursework. Those who immediately experience some challenge with regard to the expectations of school begin on a different trajectory—they experience a negative feedback loop. Worse, schools as institutions and the public at large have a nasty habit of ascribing the cause of students' failures to spurious things like a lack of parental interest, cultural deficit, or a lack of innate ability. Consequently, we tend to see less social mobility than we do social reproduction.

The third problem is a sense of earned entitlement that accompanies this ostensibly meritocratic scramble for advantage. Fighting to get to the top of the heap may detract from learning, and it certainly undermines the aim of equity, but social and economic mobility has clear benefits for the winners. And once they have won the competition, those with superlative educational records are likely to emphasize how hard they worked to compile their achievements. In other words, they tend to believe that their deserts are just. They took the tests. They made the honor roll. They graduated at the top of the class. Thus, despite the heavy hand of inequality, those who benefit from the system are often loath to give up their advantage, believing that it was solely the product of effort and ability.

Grumbling Acceptance

Of course, measures of learning *are* certainly fairer than many of the immediately available alternatives. No one wants to return to a system entirely reliant on reputation—who you know or where you went to school. The stakes are too high for individuals, for communities, and for the general public not to want some form of independent verification of the work students are doing in school. Complaints about tests being simplistic, narrow measures of learning abound, but the solution—that we should create much longer, much more elaborate (and more expensive) examinations—rarely garners much support. So, the tendency is toward tinkering to improve what we have: to create additional pieces of simplified assessment in order to create more colorful mosaics.

In short, Americans hate grades, tests, and transcripts. But we also love them at the same time. We grumble about the impact such assessment technologies have on student learning, about how they commodify the process of education, about how unfair it all is. We hate teaching to the test and grade grubbing. Students hate the pressure and the fear that much of this is permanent. Teachers hate the grind and the impingement on their autonomy.

But then many of us demand these measures. We want a "real" school that has tests and quizzes and gives grades. We want the state to exercise oversight and enforce accountability. We want students to have transcripts that they can use to move from place to place and school to school, carrying their records with them as evidence of what they've learned. We want our children to get ahead.

We grumble, but we accept it.

PART III

Sustaining Learning

False Starts and Future Prospects

6

It's a Small World after All

When we began this project, we planned to include a chapter on "international alternatives." Our thinking was that assessment of learning in the United States was likely out of step with practices across the globe. We looked forward to gathering new ideas from around the world.

We weren't completely naïve. We knew, for instance, that some countries admit students to postsecondary education only after a high-stakes national exam that essentially renders all of primary and secondary education meaningless. But we did enter our research with a significant degree of optimism. Surely, we presumed, there were entire systems that had figured things out—systems where assessment technologies were used to *enhance* learning. Mostly, however, we were wrong. When it comes to assessment of student learning, the world is a pretty small place.

One reason for this is imperialism. In case after case, we found ourselves re-learning the colonial histories of countries that had been subject to European rule in the nineteenth and twentieth centuries. As it turns out, matters like how a country grades its students, tests their knowledge, and compiles their permanent records are strongly indicative of who was in charge when their education system was created. Over and over again, we found the fingerprints of imperial powers on the instruments of assessment.

Another reason for this sameness, or "isomorphism" as a theorist would describe it, is expediency. While it may be the case that many countries across the world were once subsidiary units of imperial powers like Britain and France, it is also the case that those places have shrugged off much of the colonial past. Why, then, have assessment practices persisted? It's a complicated question, but part of the answer lies in the benefits of *legitimacy* and *legibility.* If a student aspires to attend a British university and carries with her only a collection of her prior school assignments, rather than a more typical set of qualifications, she will be at a distinct disadvantage. The British system wouldn't know how to make sense of such a portfolio. But if she presents a General Certificate of Education: Advanced Level, most British universities would know exactly how to read such a document, as would other universities around the globe. If you speak to admissions officers at highly selective American universities, they will tell you how difficult it can be to make sense of transcripts with even slightly nonstandard formats and, in the face of these difficulties, how often they solve such problem by leaning on the standardized mechanisms they have at their disposal: AP tests, TOEFL results, and SAT scores. Aspiring foreign candidates know this, too, and prepare accordingly.

Regardless of a country's experience with imperialism, most education systems around the globe feel isomorphic pressure from what might be termed globalization 2.0. As the European Centre for International Political Economy puts it: "If 'old globalization' was about goods and standard services crossing borders, 'new globalization' is about rapid economic integration through a digital exchange, technology, innovation and the organizational imitation—essentially, the globalization of ideas and knowledge."[1]

Some of this has been shepherded by major global actors like the World Bank and the Organisation for Economic Co-operation and Development (OECD). And some has happened organically, as leaders signal to the world that they are managing education in keeping with global standards. If you are trying to show other countries that you are a modern nation with a highly educated population, what better way than to have your students perform well on the OECD's standardized test, the Programme for International Student Assessment (PISA)? If you want to attract foreign investment and new high-tech jobs, what better way than by building a university system with selective admissions?

These pressures don't necessarily operate on their own. In the best cases, the stamp of legitimacy from other, more powerful countries can facilitate the adoption of what might genuinely be considered a "best practice" approach. In any case, the result is the same: considerable uniformity in assessing and recording student learning.

At the end of our research, we hadn't discovered a "model" country to point to, or a handful of reforms that might be taken up elsewhere. But we did learn something quite valuable from our look at international assessment practices. Specifically, we observed that Americans aren't alone in their frustrations with grading, rating, and ranking. It isn't as though students, families, and educators around the world are pleased with the status quo. Instead, they have substantive concerns about grades, test scores, and transcripts—concerns that are very much in line with those voiced by stakeholders in the United States.

There are a few promising practices that we make note of in this chapter. We highlight them fully aware that one of the central arguments of the book is that assessment practices are deeply embedded in the school systems and the societies that create them. Some practices, especially ones that are cultural rather than organizational, are very difficult to transplant from one environment to another. Even so, these practices, along with some of the US-based alternatives we discuss in Chapter 7, are still valuable to consider because they remind us that more balanced approaches to assessment are feasible in the real world. Mostly, however, we find that the barriers we identify in the United States are common across the globe.

In sourcing information for this chapter, we did what most scholars do: we went to the library. We learned a lot from those trips, but we also worried that we weren't getting a complete picture. First, the literature tends to privilege European countries. Moreover, as English speakers, we wondered what we were missing that we couldn't even search for. And finally, we had concerns about how current our information was. In light of this, we also reached out to roughly sixty secondary school teachers from around the world. These educators, former participants in the Fulbright Teaching Excellence and Achievement program, are recognized leaders who, as a part of their Fulbright grants, spend six weeks in the United States at graduate schools of education. Fluent in English, expert in their home contexts, and willing to indulge us, these educators offered us a better view of what is actually happening in assessment around the globe. We make no claims about how globally representative their perspectives are, but they need not be—the value of their input is in illuminating the everyday practices of schools in their home countries.

"Real" School and the Colonial Footprint

One explanation for the lack of variety we see in assessment practices around the world is fairly straightforward: colonialism. Most readers familiar with world history since 1400 know that several European nation-states established international empires around the globe and proceeded to act out their colonial ambitions well into the twentieth century. Most will also be familiar with global independence movements, which successfully expelled colonial governments. But most have likely not considered the particular challenge of scrubbing a society of its colonial residue.

As it turns out, many nations actively sought to *maintain* education systems—including assessment practices—that had been established by colonial powers. Even if they hadn't wished to maintain them, such systems would have posed a significant challenge to overhaul. Large-scale change in an enterprise as widespread and culturally embedded as education is quite difficult. Not surprisingly, most countries did not simply raze their existing school systems after the withdrawal of colonial governance. Instead, they generally accepted existing structures and worked to make them more reflective of local values and aims.

Consider the case of Cameroon, which was colonized by Germany before being invaded by the British and French during World War I. For several decades, France administered Cameroon as a colony and then as a part of the so-called French Union. After independence in 1960, Cameroon did not simply dump the elements of the education system that had been established under French rule. They sought to expand access, certainly, as well as to create more empowering curricula. But many procedural and infrastructural elements remained firmly in place, including those related to assessment. Today, students in most of modern Cameroon are graded on a 0–20 basis, just as students in France are. Like their French counterparts, students in Cameroon who wish to pursue higher education sit for exams and earn a baccalaureate diploma of secondary education (*diplôme de bachelier de l'enseignement du second degré*). And those not bound for universities can pursue vocational education at technical colleges, where they can earn a variety of certificates, including the baccalaureate of secondary education—technical and professional (*baccalauréat de l'enseignement secondaire—technique et professionel*).

Of course, not all of Cameroon was administered by the French. While that was true for most of the country, the southwest region of modern Cameroon was controlled by the British, as was a northwest region that today is part of Nigeria. Thus, whereas most of modern Cameroon speaks French, populations in those regions colonized by the British continue to speak English. In Anglophone Cameroon, students do not pursue the French *baccalauréat*. Instead, they strive for O Level ("Ordinary") and A Level ("Advanced") certificates—just as their British counterparts do.

The story is much the same to Cameroon's north, where its neighbor, Nigeria, was administered as a British protectorate across the first half of the twentieth century. Recognizing education as "an important factor in colonial control," British administrators in Nigeria sought to improve schools run by missionaries, create a new system of government-run schools, and establish general education policies.[2] And across all of this work, the British simply looked to their own system for inspiration. Chiefly, the British sought to educate Nigerians to take colonial posts as assistants for the various departments of government and commercial houses. And for their part, Nigerians often wanted what they perceived as "real" universities that would maintain familiar standards and grant them access to "degrees that would be universally recognized."[3]

Today in Nigeria, students sit for O Level exams at the end of high school, seeking to earn O Level certificates. After that, those who are university bound pursue an additional two years of schooling in the hopes of earning A Level certificates. If we were to depart from Lagos on the Trans-Sahara Highway and drive continuously for several days (with a couple of ferry rides tacked on), we might find something quite similar in London: students striving for their O Levels and A Levels. The only difference would be that while Nigeria's students would know quite well that they are participating in a British system, students in England would likely be completely unaware of their counterparts, several thousand miles south, playing a very similar game.

Why do Nigeria and Cameroon continue to mimic their former colonial governors? One reason is that they have lived with these systems for generations. Whatever the feelings of Nigerians and Cameroonians about the British and the French, their views of "real" schools are shaped by decades of experience.[4] A "real" school in Nigeria is one that culminates in O Levels and A Levels; it includes high-stakes exams that yield particular kinds of certificates. In Francophone Cameroon, a "real" school gives grades, just as in Anglophone Cameroon—grades that come in 1–20 format, rather than A–F format. And it culminates in a baccalaureate diploma. When people in these countries move through the system, they become acculturated to particular structures and practices that soon enough become "normal." When their children enter the schools, parental conceptions of normalcy then shape what they expect their children will be exposed to. As one study of Cameroon put it: "old habits die hard."[5]

There is also another reason why people from former colonies might continue to use assessment systems originally introduced by colonial governments: access. When Nigerians complete their A Level exams, they are participating in a shared system with other British Commonwealth countries. Their certificates are a recognized currency that can be used to study beyond the borders of Nigeria or Africa. Francophone Cameroonians, likewise, have continued to advocate for alignment with French schools because, in the words of one observer, "the ultimate aim of most students was to end up in French universities and professional schools."[6]

Isomorphism and the New Globalization

In addition to this history of colonialism, there is a long history of countries across Europe mimicking, if not outright copying, each other's schooling practices. Beginning in the nineteenth century, developing a school system came to be seen as the hallmark of a modern state—a sign that a nation had a mechanism to produce citizens and the capacity to administer large-scale processes. These were important outward signs of power and legitimacy. The more that having school systems became associated with modernity, the more that new and emerging states sought to create them. These ideas spread throughout the nineteenth and early twentieth centuries, as emerging countries emulated the formal school structures of their established counterparts.[7]

This trend became even more pronounced during the Cold War. The struggle between the United States and the Soviet Union for global supremacy may have divided the world, but it unified the countries on either side of the so-called Iron Curtain. In Western Europe, for instance, allies began to organize their educational programs around concepts like "human capital," often with assistance from newly founded international organizations like the OECD and the World Bank.[8] Collectively, they advanced the notion that a country was only as strong as its stock of human capital—the collective talents of the people living there—and that the best way to develop that was through formal education. For those countries still in the process of developing their school systems, showing a commitment to these values meant developing education systems similar in organization, form, and content to those operating in Western Europe and the United States.

For countries in Western Europe and the United States, this meant cultivating ways to focus attention, both inside and outside of schools, on the development of human capital. In the United States, the National Assessment of Educational Progress (NAEP) was introduced during this period—as the educational equivalent of the country's gross domestic product.[9] This domestic effort was mirrored at the international level with the creation of PISA, which was intended to measure and track progress toward these goals at a global scale. To participate in PISA, and, in turn, to have a country's school system evaluated in these terms, was to demonstrate to these values.

The intertwining of geopolitics and the creation of a global system of educational governance and assessment during the Cold War had a number of important consequences. First, it sustained the isomorphic pressure to develop school systems organized in ways considered legitimate and legible to the West.[10] Second, it added a new universalizing goal to education systems. While the meaning and character of citizenship was particular to a country, the development of human capital was seemingly universal. The embrace of human capital as at least one of the primary goals of schooling implied that different countries, despite their considerable historical, cultural, and political differences, shared a common goal of increasing economic productivity. How else can we explain the primary output of the PISA testing regime, which is not an analysis of the effectiveness of various curricula or the value of certain pedagogical approaches, but a simple ranked list of countries by their test scores? The value of these rankings wouldn't make any sense if we thought that participating countries had fundamentally different education systems with fundamentally different goals. As with the ranking table in any sports league, the table implies that these are all the same *kinds* of teams competing against each other to be the best at a common activity. Since the Cold War, school systems in countries around the world have agreed that they are competing in a common game of producing human capital.

One doesn't have to look very hard for evidence that this way of viewing schools has become part of the basic grammar of schooling—a conventional way of viewing and talking about schools. One need only consider how results of international tests are greeted by the American press to see the extent to which the United States has embraced the underlying universalizing view that all schools in all countries are fundamentally the same. When American students score lower than their counterparts around the world, the headlines—"It Just Isn't Working: PISA Test Scores Cast Doubt on U.S. Education Efforts"; "U.S. Students Fail to Make Gains Against International Peers"—make it clear that this is a cause for concern because students everywhere are in direct competition with each other.[11] If we want to be the best, we should look at the success of our competitors around the world.

If students everywhere can be ranked on a single examination, and test results can be the basis for judgments about the quality of a country's schools, it follows that there must be lessons to be drawn and practices to be borrowed from other countries' successes. Hence another brand of headline that inevitably accompanies each round of international test scores, illustrated by examples like "What Singapore Can Teach the U.S. About Education" and "What Americans Keep Ignoring About Finland's School Success."[12] The message embedded in these stories is that there are practices in use around the world that, if only Americans would wake up to them, would produce a similar level of success at home. Such articles are never filled with detailed analyses of the appropriateness of these foreign practices for American teachers, students, or schools. The value of any particular practice stems, instead, from the country's position above us in the rankings; the value of adopting the practice, therefore, requires little additional justification.

While PISA scores don't measure anything like school quality or effectiveness, the attention given to PISA scores helps explain why educators, citizens, and lawmakers believe that there is a right and a wrong way to do schooling, and that there is a right and wrong way to assess, communicate, and record learning in schools.[13] Adopting the practices of other countries ranked higher in the PISA rankings—even if those practices are ill-suited for the United States or are likely to be poorly implemented in a radically different context—is nevertheless a surefire way to show that lawmakers and policy elites are taking school performance seriously. After several decades and cycles of these recurring, internationally driven pressures, it is not surprising that systems have come to look more similar than different. Today, countries across the globe have more assessment practices in common than ever before, and that trend is likely to continue.

International Dissatisfaction

Based on our engagement with educators from around the world, it was difficult to avoid two conclusions:

1) There is a great deal more similarity than difference in the way that we assess, communicate, and record student learning in our school systems.
2) No one is especially thrilled about the current state of things.

At best, grades, ratings, and rankings are perceived as necessary evils. At worst, they are seen as active deterrents to student learning. Far from an outlier or a recalcitrant laggard in its school practices, the United States looks decidedly unremarkable when viewed alongside its international peers.

When we asked educators to describe for us how student learning was measured in their countries, the answers could just as easily have been provided by a group of American educators. The teachers described some combination of teacher-generated homework, tests, and quizzes—formative and summative evaluations—overlaid by an interlocking set of standardized evaluations emanating from local school councils, national governments, and universities. This wasn't true for *most* of the international teachers we asked; it was true for *all of them.*

That said, there was variation in degree. While using nearly identical technologies—grades, tests, and transcripts—there were differences in the precise combination of elements and weights. For instance, in Zambia, a national examinations council creates summative evaluations for students across the entire country. A student's scores on the national examinations are combined with the evaluation of the local school: 75 percent of a student's marks are based on the national examination and 25 percent on the school grade. A teacher in Cambodia offered a window into how she calculates a student's grade in her class: attendance 10 percent, homework 20 percent, assignments 30 percent, final exam 40 percent. As an educator in Nepal explained, "observation, interview, project works, written examinations, oral tests, etc. are some major tools for assessment. Student learning is also measured by his / her regular performance in sports and extra-curricular activities." And a teacher in India offered an appraisal that would hit close to home for many: "Mostly student learning is measured with the help of traditional paper-pencil tests; most assessment is writing-based where students are expected to reproduce memorized information and there is little scope for original / creative / critical thinking."

Whatever variation existed among the types of assessment or the weight placed on them, there was virtual unanimity about how information about student progress in school is communicated with families: progress reports and report cards. Whether these reports are presented as physical objects to be carried home by students or conveyed via online portals, all our respondents indicated that report cards were common practice. Some indicated that there were other more elaborate practices for communicating with parents. Parent-teacher conferences are common, as are other structural mechanisms for communicating between schools and families. An educator in Oman, for instance, explained that there were four channels available to educators who were interested in communicating about student progress with parents: parents' councils, parent school visits, report cards, and final grade reports. On the whole, however, we once more saw a story of sameness.

The uniformity in conveying student progress to parents and students is matched by the uniformity in the messaging about the stakes involved for students in these evaluations. The sense of competitiveness for college admissions in the United States may lead Americans to forget how much is at stake for students in other countries around the world. A Vietnamese educator reminded us of the pressure of piecing together a flawless record to ensure access to higher education and better opportunities. As she put it, "the majority of students as well as their parents have considered their grades at school as a decisive factor affecting their success in life." In many countries, university entrance examinations, whether given as a single national examination or by individual universities, are the *sole factor* determining admission; the pressure surrounding student performance on these examinations is commensurate with the stakes.

In many countries, students' scores on university entrance examinations determine not just whether they can enter university, but what they will study when they get there. For instance, an educator from Iraq explained that "a student's score on the standardized test (Ministerial Exam) determines their admission in universities and institutes and this admission determines their opportunities in life after graduation. All College of Medicine graduates are appointed directly after finishing their classes and they are well paid, but graduates of the College of Administration and Economics and some others can hardly find a job in the government sector regardless of their grades in their courses." Another teacher from Iraq explained, "the Ministry of Higher Education and Scientific Research controls placement, not only in universities / vocational schools but also in courses."

One notable exception was provided by a teacher who offered a reminder that accepting school achievement as a criterion for career opportunity and advancement is not an inevitability. There are alternatives. "We have noticed paradoxical practices. Sometimes the best student is left behind when it comes to job opportunities and the worst students are hired to the best companies and job positions," she explained. "We have seen a lot of corruption when it comes to job opportunities. This situation leads to demotivation. Students know that even if they do great at school, if they don't have powerful links they will rarely get job opportunities."

Though many of our respondents talked about the considerable pressure to get the grades and / or test scores needed in order to qualify for university admission, or acceptance into specific area of study, it is worth noting that there is considerable variation in the culture of competition among colleges and universities in different countries around the world. Americans don't give much thought to the idea that students compete with each other for admission and that universities, in turn, compete with each other to secure the "best" students. This overlapping competition involving both students and universities competing with each other for prestige can have the effect of diversifying the entrance criteria for admission. For some schools, an emphasis on having students with the highest scores and GPAs becomes the basis for claims about the university's elite status. But for others, the adoption of alternative criteria or the deemphasizing of scores can be a point of distinction, too.

In countries with either clear university hierarchies or limited institutional autonomy for universities, this kind of competition and differentiation is not possible. But there are other countries— Switzerland, Australia, Germany, Austria, and Canada, among others—which have historically allowed for comparatively little differentiation and competition among their institutions of higher education. While there are still competitive pressures to get into a postsecondary institution, the competition to get into the "best university" or the "best program" is lessened considerably. Instead, students are most likely to attend the closest school that provides the area of study they want to pursue. In Europe, the recent adoption of the Bologna Process, designed to make it easier for students in participating countries to apply to and attend universities in other countries, has opened up more opportunities for higher education without creating more competitive pressures.

Given the similarities in the use of assessment and grades to motivate students to do well in school, and the use of tests and grades to make high-stakes decisions about placement in higher education, it is perhaps not surprising that when we asked educators what they would like to see changed about their countries' assessment practices, we received the same answers we had heard countless times from educators in the United States. Many were dead set on eliminating standardized assessments. But many more simply hoped that the content and form of such tests would evolve. As a teacher from Mozambique explained, "teachers are forced to stick on the use of multiple choice tests because at the end of each term or school year the students are forced to sit for a state multiple choice test or national final exam. I don't see much productivity in applying multiple choice tests and exams. I would change this situation because at the end of the cycle we find that our students just learnt how to memorize."

Others sought more categorical changes in the kinds of assessments used. A Tunisian educator would urge leaders in his country to have "less interest in marks and more focus on projects as an effective way of assessment" because "projects are a continuous process that reflects whether a learner is really benefiting from their learning." An educator from Cameroon, similarly, hoped the school system would move away from grades and exams and instead "create a portfolio for each learner and make them carry out [a] project that will reflect what they can actually do because tests and exams are often not a true reflection of students' performances in real-life."

And finally, others wished for a total reconceptualization of how student achievement is assessed. One respondent from Ghana thought that the assessment system should be turned from individual achievement to community strengthening: "Assessment systems only emphasize good grades so students don't get inspiration to think out of the box. As there is no grade for doing community work, students don't feel they [should] do it. I believe they should do community work to become a sensible citizen of the country and globally." Another teacher from Bangladesh went even further, saying: "I do not want any examination or report card for assessment because in my thinking education should be focused on learning with joy . . . I think a teacher is capable of assessing students' learning and skill so there is no need to take a central examination."

As is apparent from these brief glimpses of global assessment, teachers around the world share not only many of the same practices, but also many of the same concerns about how student learning is assessed. Seeing how assessment technologies foster extrinsic motivation, create perverse incentives for teachers and students, and reduce learning to memorization, these educators imagine many of the same solutions that their American counterparts have advocated for: moving away from multiple-choice exams, fostering student mastery, reducing the stakes associated with assessments, and developing more nuanced and holistic formats to demonstrate learning. These were not the messages that we were expecting to receive when we sent out our requests for feedback. But they serve as a powerful reminder that in a globalized system of education, educators everywhere are grappling with the same challenges and seeking ways to sustain student learning.

Promising Practices

Though the primary conclusion of our search abroad for new insights and approaches was that educators everywhere are doing their best to muddle through a problematic global culture of assessment, that doesn't mean there aren't some divergent practices worth highlighting. The practices we feature here are not the only ones we could have chosen. Instead, we selected them because they offer clear attempts to target and address challenges that are central to the struggles of teachers and school leaders around the world to mitigate the effects of our assessment practices on student learning.

Of particular concern for our teacher respondents, and to so many educators around the world, is the way students experience grades as their first encounter with quantification of their learning. Grading practices—that is, the scale (A–F, 1–100, etc.), frequency, and emphasis placed on them—vary across countries more than any other element of countries' assessment systems. And that variation has preserved some promising practices that are worth highlighting.

New Zealand, for instance, has opted to communicate progress toward its National Certificate of Educational Achievement (NCEA) in secondary schooling through the use of a series of "achievement levels." To reach each of the NCEA levels, students must achieve a certain number of credits. And to earn their credits, students must pass a set of unit examinations and achievement standards. While this might sound rather conventional—students acquire credits, the accumulation of credits leads to a grade, and eventually, degree attainment—the country takes the rather unique approach of having unit standards assessed on an achieved / not achieved basis. Thus, the unit examinations operate like many competency-based standards here in the United States and elsewhere.

In many contexts, the implementation of competency-based or pass / fail standards helps reduce competition and gaming—re-centering student attention away from accumulating a sufficient number of points to achieve their desired grade and toward competency at the task. In addition to the binary assessment of its unit standards, the New Zealand NCEA system includes a slightly more elaborated four-tier system (not achieved, achieved, merit, excellence) for assessing the degree to which students have met the country's achievement standards. The multiple levels of distinction, like the multiple levels of the NCEA system, is clearly a compromise position on the role of assessments: it collapses grades in some areas into a simple binary, while still preserving the elements of a competition that is necessary to allow students to seek higher degrees of recognition. This compromise approach is especially intriguing because it reflects, in our view, a pragmatic assessment of the role of schools in modern society.

New Zealand is not alone in this general approach. Norway, likewise, opts to make clear distinctions about how grades operate in different areas of schooling. For instance, there are no grades given in primary schools in Norway. Instead, teachers in Norwegian schools write comments to students and their parents documenting progress and areas in need of improvement. This approach in early elementary school gives way to more traditional forms of grading in lower secondary school (roughly equivalent to American middle schools) and upper secondary school. Norway, like the United States, has a highly decentralized education system, which creates tensions between the prerogatives of local teachers and schools on the one hand, and the country's national educational aims on the other—tensions that increased following the perceived low performance of the nation's students on the 2001 PISA examination. While teachers continue to have flexibility in their approach, and many indicate a preference for progressive teaching practices, the clear emphasis on learning objectives and national attention to performance on international assessments produces conflicting tensions.[14]

Several countries have also developed useful alternative practices around the role of standardized tests in their systems. As many commentators have noted, while American lawmakers have opted to make standardized testing a part of the fabric of every school year at nearly every grade, Finland has opted for a radically different approach. In Finland, there are no standardized tests during students' ordinary schooling. It is only when students finish secondary school and must take the college entrance examination that they encounter a standardized test of any real consequence.

Given how wedded US education policy has become to the use of standardized tests and how deeply embedded testing is in our schooling culture, it may be hard to imagine lawmakers in the United States (or in many other countries) suddenly moving to adopt the Finnish approach of no testing. In that case, considering the evolution of testing policies in a country that has been wedded to the use of standardized testing might, therefore, be more instructive.

Recently, Singapore undertook an effort to reduce the intense competition around standardized assessment by revising the way it grades and ranks. Under the prior system, students took four examinations and the scores from those examinations were added together. With more than two hundred possible aggregate scores, the system ranked students based on small distinctions—transforming minor variations in test performance into differences with major life consequences. Under the new system, students can earn a performance level 1–8 for each of the four examinations (a score of 90 and above earns a 1; 85–89 earns a 2; 80–84 earns a 3; etc.). The result is that students now achieve one of twenty-nine possible aggregate scores. Though it is too soon to assess how well the change is working, the country hopes this "flatter" ranking system will reduce the pressure on students by eliminating the overly fine differentiation in the ranking system.[15] Removing such fine distinctions, or thinking about which distinctions are absolutely necessary to allow the system to operate, is a useful prompt for lawmakers and school officials in any context. While twenty-nine different scores is still, in our view, quite an elaborated ranking system, it is nevertheless notable that a country like Singapore undertook this reform in effort to tone down the emphasis on standardized testing.

Finally, when it comes to recording grades for the sake of long-haul communication, there are a number of different approaches that seek to de-weaponize the long-term impact of a semester's worth of feedback. As we noted already, many of our respondents reported that the way school systems in their countries de-weaponized grades was by shifting recorded evaluations of student work from teacher grades to the standardized tests taken at the end of the year or at the point of key transitions (e.g., from middle school to secondary school, or from secondary school to higher education). This creates the possibility of spaces for learning without the threat of permanent grades, though in most cases the standardized tests remain of considerable and problematic consequence. In a similar vein, countries like Finland opt not to forgo recording student grades, but instead reduce the information recorded to the bare minimum: whether a student passed or failed. In all these cases, the underlying logic is the same and worthy of consideration.

It Could Be Worse

As Americans, we are used to hearing people—parents, lawmakers, the general public—complain about the state of US schools. The subtext of many such complaints is an unstated assumption that things are certainly better somewhere else. In truth, we assumed the same ourselves. We thought this chapter would focus chiefly on the ingenious solutions developed in other countries.

Instead of finding a great variety of assessment practices, however, we mostly found a monoculture. Educators across six continents and sixty countries reported struggling with many of the same things: the gravitational weight of grading and testing in the organization of schooling, the perverse incentives for teachers to teach to and students to study for the tests, the inability of current assessment technologies to capture or convey what students are actually capable of doing. In some respects, this might seem like a depressing piece of news: there really isn't a better assessment widget out there that we can import to improve our system. But the truth is, this was always wishful thinking. The largest differences between school systems are products of the culture and politics that surround them—the impetus to revere those in the teaching profession (or at least pay them more), for instance, or the social commitment to reduce the social inequality that becomes educational inequality—and those things are virtually impossible to import.

On the flipside, knowing that there isn't an easy solution that we've simply been ignoring should offer solace and resolve to those looking to reform the practices of grading, rating, and ranking. We are all muddling through together. Globally, we are looking at the same challenges and imagining some of the same solutions, and improvements are more likely to come from adjustments to the system than from radical transformation. In fact, as we argue in the next chapter, many elements of promising improvements are already being tried in one way or another by educators in school systems across the United States. The problem is not that we haven't thought of the right ways to rebalance our system, but that we haven't given enough attention to how to combine these alternatives in a way that makes for meaningful change without sacrificing the core functions of assessing learning in schools.

7

Homegrown Experiments

Around the world, the quantification of student learning has created problems that frequently make assessment more harmful than helpful. In response, educators have developed a range of creative alternatives designed to minimize unintended consequences and restore the rightful place of learning to our schools.

In this chapter, we look at a handful of experimental approaches that have gained something of a foothold in the United States. But this is not a story of solutions waiting to be taken to scale. Instead, this chapter particularly highlights the limitations of these efforts. In doing so, it emphasizes the importance of addressing the many problems posed by current approaches to assessment, and especially of getting to the root causes of those problems.

The table below summarizes the key challenges that we identified in Part I, as well as the primary underlying source.

Although each of the alternative approaches examined in this chapter addresses one of these problems, none do so in a manner

Table 7.1

Current Problem	Root Cause
Gaming: grading, rating, and ranking incentivize students to learn behaviors and routines that will earn them points, rather than developing knowledge and skill.	**Construct invalidity:** assessments capture something other than what they purport to capture (e.g., not mastery of a subject, but mastery of earning points).
Weaponization: assessments have significant stakes for students, teachers, and schools, which increases pressure and anxiety for teachers and students.	**Permanence:** assessment results are recorded in an unalterable form and persist long into the future.
Informational "thinness": assessments offer only a limited description of what students know and can do.	**Compression:** grading, rating, and ranking reduces information about student knowledge and skills into an easily digestible number or grade.
Extrinsic motivation: grading, rating, and ranking motivates students to acquire tokens and credentials, rather than to value the process or content of education.	**Commodification:** grading, rating, and ranking emphasizes the exchange-value of education; the symbols of learning are what have the greatest value.
Inequity: assessments treat students differently based on features other than their abilities and levels of effort, often advantaging socially and economically privileged populations.	**Manipulatability:** assessments insufficiently resist effort to influence their results via processes or strategies other than learning.

that would successfully lead to systemic transformation. Rather than offer endorsements or criticisms of these alternative approaches, then, our aim is to discuss them as miniature case studies—exploring the insights they provide and the lessons they offer about the prospects for reform. We are particularly attuned to three functions of assessment, which we have discussed previously and summarize below:

- Motivation: to produce particular responses and elicit specific behaviors from students.
- Communication: to transmit "short-haul" messages (e.g., from teacher to parents) and "long-haul" messages (e.g., from school to future employer).
- Synchronization: to promote system-level coherence and operation (e.g., proving that a student has completed one "level" of schooling and is ready for the next).

Though no one model is sufficient as a replacement for grades, tests, or transcripts, together the alternatives in this chapter highlight the kinds of practices that might be assembled in a more complete reform package—one that addresses the multiple problems of grades, ratings, and rankings, and gets to the root causes of those problems.

The Genuine Article: Authentic Assessment

One of the core challenges inherent to the way we measure and track student learning is that students end up pursuing tokens and credentials, rather than learning itself. If good grades, high test scores, and shimmering transcripts are the goal for students, then learning is an afterthought that can usually be minimized, and occasionally avoided altogether. Sometimes, of course, students are generally interested in expanding what they know and can do in a subject. Most students, however, respond to the incentives built into our assessment systems in a rational fashion: by doing the least amount of work necessary to acquire the highest value tokens.

"Authentic assessment" is a response to this problem. The goal of authentic assessment is for students to *use* the knowledge and skills that the class purportedly seeks to cultivate. Assessment guru Grant Wiggins, who coined the term "backwards planning" and coauthored the best-selling *Understanding by Design,* put it this way: "Authentic assessments require students to be effective performers with acquired knowledge." Traditional assessments, by contrast, "tend to reveal only whether the student can recognize, recall or 'plug in' what was learned out of context. This may be as problematic as inferring driving or teaching ability from written tests alone."[1]

So, rather than take a multiple-choice test to assess students' history knowledge (something no professional historian would ever be asked to do), students might be asked do something that historians *actually do*: piece together fragments from the archival record to offer an interpretation of the past. Instead of answering questions from their science textbooks, students would actually have to *do* science.

One way of describing the difference between authentic and inauthentic assessments is to talk about the psychometric concept of "validity." There are several different kinds of validity, but two in particular are important for understanding the value of authentic assessment. The first is referred to as "construct validity," which is concerned with whether a test adequately measures the concept that we are interested in assessing—scientific literacy, for instance. The more complex the construct, the more sophisticated our assessment needs to be in order for us to have confidence that we are adequately measuring what we're interested in.

A second kind of validity is referred to as "predictive validity." This type of validity is concerned with whether a student who performs well on an assessment is also likely to perform well on other measures related to a construct. For instance, we would hope that a surgeon's performance on the medical boards she must pass in order be licensed will be predictive of her future success in the operating room. That is, we hope that performance on the one challenge accurately predicts performance on the other. As much as we would like it to be, however, this isn't always the case.

It's easy to think of examples where the predictive validity of an assessment might fail because the assessment only captures a small fraction of the key construct. A multiple-choice test about driving, for instance, might tell us whether you know the meaning of road signs and lane markings, but it would not be a valid instrument for measuring the actual skill of safely operating a vehicle on a road. One could even go a step further and say that the ability of a driver to maneuver a vehicle in an empty parking lot might not predict his ability to drive safely on a busy street with traffic lights, cars, and pedestrians. As Wiggins put it: "'Test validity' should depend in part upon whether the test simulates real-world tests of ability."[2] For advocates of authentic assessment, the best way to ensure predictive validity is to eliminate, or reduce as much as possible, the distance between the form a construct takes on an assessment and the form it takes in the real world.

People will often argue—usually in response to complaints about teachers "teaching to the test"—that we need to develop "tests worth teaching to." More authentic assessments are usually what people have in mind when they raise this argument. Teaching to the test is usually effective because the tests only measure a small and often predictable aspect of a construct. By learning how to do a particular kind of algebra problem, say, or how to guess effectively on a particular kind of reading comprehension question, students can increase the likelihood of improving their test performance without greatly improving their abilities in algebra or reading.

If authentic assessments have a higher degree of validity, they would—at least in theory—be less prone to this kind of gaming. Or, more precisely, gaming wouldn't actually undermine the intended learning objectives. After all, a cook who learns how to make a dish only to pass a test will still know how to make the dish. The distance between gaming and learning, in such a case, becomes very small. By contrast, a cook who stays up all night memorizing facts about seafood, and whose mother helps him write his essay about shellfish, may ace the exam without being able to prepare an edible meal. Such assessments, as in this latter example, are merely games to be played for a grade or a score—a challenge tangential to learning. Our aspiring chef might still be motivated to improve his technique, but the assessment system certainly isn't encouraging it.

The authenticity of assessment matters. Indeed, there has been a push across a number of subjects to try to make assessments less rigid and more authentic. One of the most notable examples of this is the shift in examinations for prospective teachers. A new generation of teacher licensure examinations has moved away from multiple-choice-based examinations of teacher knowledge and toward assessments of prospective teachers' facility with teaching actual students in actual classrooms. In one widely adopted assessment, prospective teachers must submit video clips of their classroom teaching, along with essays explaining and analyzing their pedagogical approach to the lessons.[3] Likewise, the Next Generation Science Standards (NGSS) is an ongoing effort to remake science standards, curriculum, and assessment in a way that provides students with a more authentic view of what scientists and engineers do. As indicated in the assessment rubrics for the new standards, the goal is to move away from assessments that focus on getting the right answer, and toward "student sense-making of phenomena or designing solutions . . . as a window into student understanding," which is developed ideally through "*direct* (preferably firsthand, or through media representations) experience with a phenomenon or problem."[4]

Authenticity sounds pretty good, so what's the downside? Who would possibly advocate for *inauthentic* assessments?

While in the abstract authenticity is better than inauthenticity, in practice not everything that happens in a school setting can be authentic. And even when we can agree that we want to strive for authenticity, agreeing on what constitutes "authentic" practice or what elements of a complex domain ought to be prioritized for authentic assessment can be an extremely challenging problem.

The closer a student is to the end of her training, the easier it is to create and evaluate authentic practice. A doctoral student completing her PhD in physics has both the knowledge and sophistication to be assessed by experts on the actual everyday practices of a physicist in a variety of "real world" settings. But what would it mean to assess an elementary school student, a middle school student, or even a high school student in these practices?

The history of science education offers useful, if slightly discouraging, insight into this challenge. When science first entered the high school curriculum in the nineteenth century, it was as a technical subject that emphasized laboratory work for the value it placed on precise measurement, which was thought to provide students with mental discipline and moral uplift. But laboratory work was soon seen as expensive and largely irrelevant to most students. As a result, it was replaced, in part thanks to John Dewey, by a broader and more widely applicable view of science built around the five-step scientific method that most of us are familiar with—the one that begins with an observation and ends with an experiment. The five-step method was a way to teach students not only about scientific practice, but also a general problem-solving technique that could be applied to everyday problems.

This view became immensely popular, but it, too, came in for criticism from scientists who objected that the sort of problem solving that might be authentic to students' lives was actually an *inauthentic* representation of expert scientific practice. There was no such thing as *the* scientific method, scientists complained; things looked different depending on the specific scientific discipline. Besides, they argued, the scientific method rarely proceeded neatly across five steps. The process was much messier, less linear, and more iterative than implied by the exercises performed by students in most classrooms. Classroom lab experiments never failed or produced inconclusive data like experiments in a real laboratory; quite the contrary, the whole point of a classroom science "experiment" was to demonstrate a well-known scientific construct. This dissatisfaction led to a new shift emphasizing "scientific practices." But which practices the curriculum should emphasize, which ones should be assessed, and to what end, remains a subject of major debate.[5]

The questions surrounding authentic assessment become even more complicated if we accept that most students do not take science class because we expect that they will grow up one day to be professional scientists. We want to keep that option open for them, certainly, which is often why we require students take specific subjects. But science, like most elements of the curriculum, is there because we believe there are benefits to study that extend beyond future employment prospects. Regardless of the specific subject—math, chemistry, history—proponents of specific subjects talk in terms of generic constructs like teamwork, critical thinking, problem solving, citizenship, or, most abstractly, "twenty-first-century skills." How to develop authentic assessments of these general constructs in the context of specific subjects becomes increasingly abstract and contentious the further we move into the full range of subjects taught in school.

Even if a school was able to make all of its assessments authentic, there would still be negative consequences associated with grades and transcripts. Teachers might adjust their instruction around authentic assessments, and students might learn more. But what gets recorded at the end of the semester? Probably still a letter grade on a transcript. Because of that, the stakes associated with grades don't change simply because we opt for more authentic assessments. An F will still be just as devastating for a student, and just as final. Moreover, a student's permanent record will remain just as informationally thin as it was before. Perhaps the student can speak Spanish like a native or write code like a pro; but the transcript will only tell us what grade was earned in AP Spanish Language and Culture or in Honors Computer Science.

There's one more problem to consider if classroom assessments are the only part of the assessment ecosystem to change: the lingering impact of state accountability systems. If schools continue to be ranked and rated according to their standardized test scores, and standardized tests continue to consist chiefly of machine-scored multiple-choice questions, how authentic will classroom assessments actually be? In high-scoring schools, educators might remain free to teach however they wish. But in lower-scoring schools, there will continue to be intense pressure to teach in a manner that raises standardized test scores, because decades of experience have taught teachers—quite correctly—that standardized test scores are sensitive to curricular alignment. If students aren't familiar with the way that ideas or problems will be presented on the test, their scores are likely to be lower. If the pressure to teach in a way that conforms to the tests is resisted, students might learn in a manner that cannot be captured by state agencies, which might lead to the tragically ironic outcome of the state labeling a school with robust authentic assessment practices as "ineffective." A state office of education could, of course, try to encourage authenticity by redesigning its accountability system around different kinds of tests. But this almost certainly means vastly increasing the cost and the time involved in carrying out the assessment.

Food for Thought

What dynamics in our current assessment system does authentic assessment highlight? First, its core insight and critique of the current system is that assessment must be tightly linked to our desired outcomes in a subject, such that if a student succeeds on the assessment there is a greater likelihood that he or she will actually possess the knowledge and skill signaled by their score. There is a lot to learn about minimizing gaming by focusing on validity.

At the very least, even if students were not always doing "authentic" work in their classes, course grades should probably not be an accumulation of points that fail to reflect core competencies. If the class is called "Showing Up on Time, Raising Your Hand, and Doing All of Your Busywork," then it makes sense to include participation and homework in a course grade. But in most cases, it probably doesn't. If it is possible to succeed in the course without developing the core competencies, or, equally important, if it is possible to *fail* in a course while having mastered the core competencies, the assessment is incentivizing something other than learning. It is not just that a student in such a classroom would be assessed on the wrong things, but also that the assessments would communicate to the student the wrong things about the class. Students are extremely savvy when it comes to discerning what's valued in a course. When a course incentivizes busywork, students become motivated—or at least incentivized—to do that busywork. Some people will argue that students' natural curiosity and motivation to learn are almost certainly more likely to be piqued by authentic representations of subjects and the use of real-life, open-ended problems. But one can be agnostic on this issue and still agree that if students are going to receive cues about the kind of work that is important in school, those cues should point to substantive knowledge and skills.

In terms of communication, authentic assessments also underscore that we should be thinking more carefully about how to tell proximate communities (e.g., families and educators) and distant communities (e.g., colleges and employers) what students know and can do. The complexity and sophistication of authentic assessment within a given classroom easily can be lost if the only by-product of that experience is the traditional letter grade on a student transcript or a traditional number score on a state-level standardized assessment. Such practices do not eliminate the value of the learning experience for the student, but they do reduce enthusiasm for embracing truly authentic assessments.

Still, determining how best to communicate about student performance on authentic assessments is harder than it might at first appear. Most authentic practices are composed of an array of elements including mastery of concepts, skills, and processes; so which ones should be recorded and reported? And which ones can be rightly considered abilities of individual students, as opposed to characteristics of particular classrooms or groups of students?

There is likely to be a sliding scale between the level of authenticity, the level of student, and the desired level of specificity in the record. The closer someone is to a decision point about a student's competence with an authentic practice, the more detail is likely to be desired; even then, it might depend on audience. A teacher licensing board or a principal hiring new staff might want to know a prospective teacher's scores on each of the fifteen licensure examination rubrics; parents of students in that teacher's classroom, by contrast, might simply want to know that the teacher is certified.

Finally, in terms of synchronization, there are real trade-offs to consider. Grading, rating, and ranking functions, in part, to stitch together a decentralized system of semiautonomous schools, districts, colleges, and universities. Yet, because systemic coherence requires standardized units, courses, and measures of learning, the pursuit of synchronization often comes at the expense of authentic inquiry. Opting for more holistic assessments of abilities might mean wider variation in individual skill development across classes, as not every authentic inquiry or assessment is likely to emphasize precisely the same set of skills. This could potentially pose problems as students get further along in their academic careers. Moreover, given the high stakes currently associated with demonstrating student competencies to external audiences—colleges, employers, and the wider public—an external evaluation system that does not recognize, let alone reward, the kind of risk taking associated with a shift to authentic assessment is likely to create disincentives to adoption.

This is why authentic assessment is often associated with private schools, which need to distinguish themselves from public schools and other competitors. It is also why, in the context of higher education, authentic assessment is often associated with professional and vocational licensing programs—programs in which "authentic tasks" are easier to identify, and where the rewards for students and programs investing in these practices are also more tightly aligned.

Ideally, we would create an evaluation system that could accommodate both open inquiry and the need for clear standards. But the evaluation system needed in order to monitor such a system would have to be many, many degrees more sophisticated than any currently in operation inside schools, districts, or state offices around the United States (or around the world). How to observe and evaluate complex learning outcomes across classrooms, but without specific classroom contexts, is something we have yet to figure out.[6]

Show, Don't Tell: Portfolio Assessments

As with many alternatives, the idea of collecting actual student work, rather than symbols of that work, is an old one. The thinking behind such an effort is that the work, itself, contains far more information than a traditional letter grade. Perhaps even better, it is produced during the normal course of the school year and therefore does not require the time and effort set aside for traditional standardized assessments. This premise is behind the effort by states, districts, and schools to experiment with so-called portfolio assessments. Derived from the realm of creative arts, the portfolio is intended to offer an opportunity for students and teachers to provide examples of work demonstrating a student's range of skills, interests, and abilities, which can then be shared and evaluated.

The idea to experiment with portfolios gained steam following the first sustained political movement for statewide standardized assessments in the 1970s. The minimum competency movement, as the effort came to be known, stressed the importance of basic competencies and, in many places, sought to evaluate them via multiple-choice tests. In the highest stakes instances, states like Florida conditioned students' diplomas on their ability to pass these assessments. As with so many large-scale encounters with standardized assessments, the minimum competency movement struck many as incentivizing the wrong things when it came to both teacher instruction and student learning. In response, states like Vermont and Kentucky, and even the federal government through the National Assessment of Educational Progress, began experimenting with whether portfolio-based assessment could redirect student and teacher energies in more productive ways.

The theoretical benefits of moving to a portfolio model are fairly obvious. The format itself is flexible, providing room for ownership and creativity among students and teachers. And, like authentic assessments, the products offered up for examination in portfolios can be more organic by-products of the course, at least as compared to traditional standardized assessments. This means that the elements of the course can reflect both a wide range of learning outcomes as well as a longer and more sustained amount of work on the part of the student, especially when compared to the range of outcomes and the amount of time allowed for a traditional standardized test.

As with authentic assessments, the incentive for students gaming their way to a good grade is also reduced, because the elements contained in the portfolio can be more tightly or explicitly linked to the intended learning outcomes of the course. Time that students invest in improving their portfolios is, therefore, time well spent.

Moreover, because the final products included in the portfolio can go through multiple drafts, the cost of "failing" is zero. Portfolio based assessments, then, can be both "formative" (offering feedback to students about their progress) and "summative" (for the purpose of evaluation) at the same time. This allows teachers to emphasize the importance of process and revision, and, many would argue, more resembles learning and work challenges people face outside of school contexts.

The benefits of portfolio assessments, however, are also the source of many of their challenges. The flexibility of the portfolio, if utilized, almost by definition means a lack of standardization. This creates a real challenge when it comes to any form of external evaluation of portfolio products. In a writing portfolio, how does one compare a collection of poems to a report evaluating the accuracy of historical claims made by elected leaders? Of course, the content of a portfolio can be specified in considerable detail—the number of items, the content and form of those items, and so on. But each requirement limits the discretion of teachers and the freedom of students. What conclusions should an evaluator draw when students opt to put different kinds of work products in their portfolios when those products vary considerably in difficulty or complexity? Did students not take on a more ambitious task because they were not invited to do so by their teacher? Or did they choose a more straightforward task because they did not feel ready to take on a bigger challenge?

There is also the subtler problem of considering how individual effort is actually reflected in the portfolio products. To the extent that students get differing levels of feedback, support, or direct assistance from their teachers and their families, how can someone fairly evaluate a student's work? We take it for granted that a standardized test requires students to produce work "on demand" with no assistance or help from anyone else. Though this is not how most work products are produced outside of school contexts, the notion that students are evaluated on what they can produce in a controlled setting is fundamental to our schools, especially when that evaluation has high stakes and when external inequities are so considerable.

These problems are not just theoretical. A comprehensive evaluation of the efforts to introduce portfolio assessments in Vermont and Kentucky found that while teachers viewed portfolios as largely a positive development, and reported adjusting their instruction to match the portfolio goals, they also reported that the time required to score portfolios was considerable—80 percent of Vermont teachers believed the task was too time consuming even after three years of experience with it.[7] Even more formidable than the time involved in scoring was the challenge of achieving consistency in the scores assigned to portfolios. Evaluators were often in disagreement with each other, raising questions about whether the portfolios could be accurately scored. And though aggregating scores across all the elements of the rubric into a single rating improved agreement between raters, it also eliminated the value and complexity of the assessment score provided. These problems were compounded when teachers, as in Kentucky, were asked to provide an initial evaluation of their own students' portfolios. The gap between the teachers' evaluations of their own students and the scores assigned by independent evaluators was considerable.[8]

After studying the experience of these states with portfolio assessments, the general assessment of scholars, including testing expert Dan Koretz, was dispiriting. With respect to the ability of portfolios to "provide, educators, students and parents, policymakers and the public at large with specific types of information about students' performance," Koretz observed, "clearly, the evidence that has accrued to date from large-scale portfolio assessments in the U.S. is not encouraging in this regard." In particular, the experiments "failed to overcome one of the most basic and essential procedural hurdles—obtaining consistent scoring of student work." He added that "even those that have attained reasonably consistent scoring have not produced evidence that the resulting scores provide a valid basis for the specific inferences users base on them, such as judgements about the relative level of performance across schools or districts."[9] As Chester E. Finn Jr., president of the Fordham Foundation and a general supporter of standardized testing, quipped, portfolio assessment "is costly indeed, and slow and cumbersome, but I think its biggest flaw as an external assessment is its subjectivity and unreliability."[10]

More recently, states have experimented with splitting the difference between portfolio assessments and external standardized assessments by incorporating both. For instance, the New York Performance Standards Consortium has a waiver from state testing in New York, allowing students in roughly three dozen public schools to take only the English language arts exam. To graduate, students need to complete performance-based assessment tasks, including an analytical essay on literature, a social studies research paper, and a science experiment. Schools can also add tasks in areas like art and foreign language. Those tasks are then externally evaluated by educators in the consortium. Ann Cook, the consortium's executive director, stresses the importance of the assessments as a signal to teachers and students of the things that are important: "We know assessments have an impact on curriculum and instruction. If you have a testing environment, teachers are going to teach to the test.

If you have a system that requires kids to write and present, then that begins to affect curriculum and instruction."[11] In a similar vein, the Advanced Placement and International Baccalaureate programs have begun to incorporate portfolios as the basis for scores in some of their courses. For instance, the AP program has three art and design courses in addition to new courses in AP Seminar, AP Research, and AP Computer Science Principles, which all require students to submit portfolios of work that can be subjected to standardized assessment.

Food for Thought

Experiments with portfolios suggest that they offer valuable and robust opportunities for short-haul communication with parents, students, and future teachers. These opportunities have only expanded with the affordances of digital technology and large-scale cloud storage, making it possible to capture and share multiple forms of student work in multiple formats (text, picture, video, etc.), with multiple audiences, and with ease. As one portfolio advocate noted, "Students can be issued an online account where work can be scanned in and collected each year. This information can be shared with parents, students, and future teachers to help inform instruction. Rather than random test scores that often don't highlight the depth of student learning, these online portfolios will be available to present classroom teachers and future ones right away."[12] Although this is promising news for supporters of portfolios, digital privacy activists have also raised some concerns about the collection of more and more data about young people.

The value of portfolio assessments for long-haul communication depends a great deal on what becomes of the products that are placed in these portfolios. If all that happens is that the portfolios are replaced with a single score or grade on a transcript, then we haven't progressed much beyond the status quo—especially when we factor in the considerable difficulties and uncertainties around scoring portfolios fairly and consistently. There are new efforts like those of the Mastery Transcript Consortium, which has sought to replace traditional transcripts with digital ones allowing students or teachers to embed work products alongside the traditional grading information. This provides the opportunity for interested parties to move between the full-scale work product and the compressed form of the evaluation with relative ease. That said, striking the right balance in the number and variety of examples included remains an important consideration.

In terms of student motivation, portfolios certainly offer opportunities for students to become fully invested in long-term substantive products that they can learn from and take pride in. As with so many elements of the classroom, whether this potential is unlocked depends a great deal on the incentives created by state policy and the ability, enthusiasm, and support of individual teachers as they seek to adapt their instruction to this new environment. If teachers do not feel supported in their work or do not feel that the time investment required to evaluate portfolios is valued and rewarded, they are unlikely to shift the instructional focus of their courses. It is easy enough for teachers to instruct students to fill their portfolios with the same assignments they've been assigning for decades.

The issue of system coherence—synchronization, as we call it—is animated by similar challenges. For three decades, policymakers have focused on identifying clear standards and assessment criteria for core subjects. But there is a clear trade-off between the level of specificity demanded by state standards and rubrics, on the one hand, and the flexibility afforded by a shift to portfolio assessments. The more we encourage teachers to lean into the opportunities for creativity provided by portfolios, the more difficult it becomes to assess them and to ensure that classes with the same title engage students in similar work. Efforts to improve systemic synchronization, therefore, might run directly counter to the ability of portfolio assessments to empower teachers and their students. This goes not only for the work and skills developed in any given course, but also for the reliability of any external evaluations. Variability in course experiences and the work produced by students in each course will likely decrease the traditional value of course transcripts and place a new burden on those who rely on them. Instead of observing a course title and grade, remote audiences will likely need to conduct their own assessment of students' work. We might consider this a good thing on balance, but it definitely represents a challenge we would have to manage and account for.

Telling Stories: Narrative Evaluations

Since its founding in the 1960s, The Evergreen State College in Washington has given narrative evaluations to students in lieu of grades. As the college's website puts it: "Narrative evaluations express the thinking that went into your work, what you completed, and the reactions of both you and your faculty members to your work. These detailed documents often provide specific examples of achievement or progress."[13]

One of the core challenges with grades, tests, and transcripts is that the information provided to the student is "thin." That is, it is compressed to facilitate long-haul travel to those beyond the immediate environments of school and family. Future employers may, in some ways, benefit from information as condensed as a GPA. But the educational community that surrounds a student—a community that includes family members and teachers at the school—generally wants far more information than numbers or letter grades can provide. Where is a student strong? What are his or her weaknesses? What are the competencies families should work to support? What should next year's teachers watch out for? None of those are answered by an A–F grade or by a score on a standardized test.

Written narratives and their oral counterparts—often referred to as "live commentary"—solve this communication problem by restoring firsthand interactions between educators and schools on the one hand, and between students and their families on the other. As a result, these short-haul communications can be vastly improved through greater informational detail—what we call informational "thickness."

Narrative evaluations can also lower the temperature on grades. Whatever teachers are *actually* trying to communicate to students, grades are often read by students as indicators of their value as individuals. An A means something along the lines of "you're great!" while an F means "you're a loser!" Just as problematically, grades often send a message that students should stop putting in so much effort—either because they're getting good grades ("you've mastered this, you're all set!") or bad ones ("you shouldn't even bother trying!"). Anything, then, to moderate these perceived messages is a win. And what better than clear language, direct from the instructor, to temper those incomplete and undesirable messages? Without a grade to distract them, students might actually read comments from their teachers, and those comments might help students understand both their strengths and their growth areas.

The most obvious obstacle to narrative assessments, of course, is time.[14] A typical public school teacher with five classes of twenty students each will have a hundred essays, projects, or problem sets to grade. Imagine that each narrative comment is a mere four sentences long: two sentences about students' strengths, and two about ways to improve. Ideally, we would want something longer, but we'll scale back our ambitions for the moment. Now try writing four model sentences about the previous paragraph; what did you like, and where could it have been stronger? It had a sense of humor—so that may have been engaging. And it was written in jargon-free prose. But it may have been a little too glib for some people's taste, and it probably overgeneralized to some extent. One or two minutes is probably about right. So, we can estimate that a stack of student work with narratives will take two to four hours.

Of course, narratives should probably be longer for end-of-course evaluations. What has a student mastered? Where is she showing promise? Where is she struggling? And what should she focus on to improve? Are there particular resources she should be seeking out, either as ways of extending mastery or building competence? And can the narrative be crafted in a way that leads to higher levels of motivation, interest in the topic, or self-confidence? Answering these questions might take five to ten minutes per student, or roughly ten to twenty hours. It adds up.

How useful is this feedback for families and students? Is it worth the day or two of teacher labor required to produce those written comments? It depends, of course, on the nature of each comment. Paragraph-length comments—the sort that private prep schools issue once per term—are sometimes too brief to really be instructive. Instead, something the length of a letter of recommendation might be necessary. But the time required for that would be borderline impossible at any level of the system. For short-haul communication, then, it probably makes sense to invest in parent-teacher conferences or direct conversations with students. These meetings might be ephemeral, but they are more likely to provide meaningful insight and they provide the opportunity for a give and take—the chance to challenge, probe, and gain greater understanding.

The other audience for such narratives would be at a greater remove—long-haul communication to other schools for the purpose of transfer or continuing education, as well as to other organizations. How would these end-of-course narratives travel to reach those audiences? Would they live on a student's transcript? And if so, what are other institutions going to make of those narrative comments? Even schools like Evergreen exist in a web that requires educational currency such as grade point averages. Long-haul communication—to graduate schools or prospective employers—demands comparability and information compression. In response to such pressures, Evergreen has to step back from its progressive stance on evaluation and move toward the status quo, transforming narratives into letter grades. Though some might see that as a way of having it both ways, others are likely to see this backtracking as reducing narrative evaluations to a gimmick. The big challenge is one that will be familiar to many teachers: if the assessment exists in both narrative and grade form, how many students will see past the grade to the narrative feedback? The answer will likely depend on the degree to which future audiences emphasize the narrative or the grade. But this only underscores the extent to which individual schools are hemmed in by their place in the larger system.

The tensions and trade-offs here are real. The University of California Santa Cruz had long prided itself on providing students narrative rather than letter grades. But the school recently took a series of steps to move away from that system—first by making grades optional for students who wanted them in addition to their narrative evaluation, then by recording grades as an accompaniment to narrative evaluations; finally, they made narrative evaluation optional, with students having to request narrative evaluations and faculty members having to assent to the request.[15] Among the reasons cited for the evolution of the grading system at UCSC was the need for students to have a GPA to calculate and report for graduate school admission, the overwhelming amount of time required to produce narrative grades, and, in the case of ballooning enrollments in introductory courses, the sheer impossibility of faculty or teaching assistants knowing the students well enough to write substantive narrative evaluations.

Food for Thought

Narrative evaluations highlight an interesting tension in the purpose of summative evaluations. While substantive, narrative feedback on individual assignments—explaining the strengths and weaknesses of a student's approach—is commonplace, the idea of providing something similar at the *conclusion* of a course requires us to ask: to what end? In terms of short-haul communication, the value of these comments could be valuable provided the content is concrete, substantive, and specific. But as anyone who has ever read a stack of letters of recommendation will attest, this may be easier said than done. The tendency toward generic, anodyne statements about "being a hard worker," "persevering through adversity," or "being a self-starter" is very high and likely to increase when the comments are produced in bulk.

The same questions could be raised about the long-haul value of the narrative comments. What is the context in which having forty narrative letters describing a student's strengths and weaknesses for each semester and each class is useful to the recipient? The notion that future recipients of a student's transcript might want the story behind the grades is already built into most admissions and interview processes: many colleges ask students to submit letters of recommendation from their teachers and, likewise, most employers and graduate schools will ask for letters of reference. It is fair to ask whether students feel equally positioned to ask professors or teachers for letters of reference or whether students have equal access to the most capable letter writers. Maybe requiring professors and instructors to produce these narrative accounts levels the playing field in some respect. But there is clearly a trade-off in terms of the quality and detail that instructors will be able to provide if they are doing them for all their students.

Would narrative evaluations change student motivation and behavior around grade seeking? It's hard to say. Narrative evaluations change the way that grades are recorded, but they don't change the structure of the course or the assignments within it. It is possible that teachers, knowing that in the end they will write a narrative evaluation, might opt to eschew all forms of letter and numerical grading in favor of narrative feedback. But this is not inherent to narrative evaluation itself. There is the other side of the coin, which is that, love them or hate them, grades are a pretty strong motivator for students to work. Take them away entirely, and you'll see what students actually think of your teaching. Now, many students aren't interested in grades because they've already received a message that school isn't for them. And many students will stop being *de-motivated* by bad grades. Still, are educators ready to dump the carrot and stick of grades?

While student motivation under narrative evaluation might be a mixed bag, the synchronization issues associated with deriving a clear interpretation of narratives are immense. While narrative evaluations, when done well, can provide lots of detail and context about a student's work in a class, those reviewing grades often want a much more straightforward assessment: is this student more accomplished than another student in the subject? Making this determination in the context of an elaborate narrative evaluation can be very challenging and can feel a little bit like parsing a coded message. Every teacher has a different style of recommendation and a different tendency toward the use of hyperbole and superlatives—one that can be difficult to ascertain without being exposed to multiple letters from the same author. Is "excellent" as high as the teacher's scale goes in rating students? Or are there greater heights—"*truly* excellent" or "one of the best in years"—that a student might ascend to? Some teachers lean into this challenge and provide a clear crosswalk for readers between the comments and more traditional rankings of students. And many schools explicitly seek this information by asking recommenders to fill out a short questionnaire offering a relative rating of an applicant's ability (e.g., top 5 percent; top 20 percent) on specific dimensions—presumably to provide the context necessary to interpret the narrative in the recommendation. Of course, to the degree that narrative evaluations require accompanying rank order information, it also undercuts the aims of moving toward narratives.

Sink or Swim: Pass / Fail and Contract Grading Systems

What if we kept grades, but still tried to de-weaponize them, as narrative comments do? Perhaps we can skip the step of writing long commentaries and instead settle for lowering the temperature by switching to a pass / fail system?

This is not a new idea. According to one source, the University of Michigan tried it as early as the 1850s.[16] But it faded as schools built the grading systems we know and loathe today. It wasn't until that system emerged fully formed—with letter grades, grade point averages, official transcripts, and so on—that people began to push back. Whatever happened to learning for the sake of learning?

Pass / fail grading reemerged in the 1960s and early 1970s.[17] And it emerged largely in higher education, where it was assumed that students were mature enough to make their own decisions about how hard to work. By 1973, more than half of American colleges and universities were offering pass / fail grading as an option.[18] By contrast, pass / fail has always been much less common at lower levels of schooling. Many people worry that, in contrast to older students who have a sense of their professional goals, younger students might not appreciate the way that early school decisions might constrain their educational opportunities later in life, especially in schools with traditional course sequencing. Students might do just well enough to pass and then find out, too late, that they aren't eligible or prepared for the next level. Requiring students to take courses for grades forestalls that possibility and ensures the extrinsic motivation of grades stays in place.

What would be the benefits of moving to pass / fail grading systems, beyond relieving the pressure on students? One argument is that students might begin taking challenging courses that otherwise could blemish their grade point averages, leading them to experiment outside their comfort zones, rather than simply pad their transcripts.[19] Another argument is that it would create space for intrinsic motivation by limiting the degree to which students can distinguish or compare themselves on the basis of earned grades. As one advocate recently asked: "Does a traditional grading system encourage students to constantly strive for excellence, a habit that, theoretically, they would maintain when they no longer receive grades?"[20] No longer motivated by "getting an A" or being the valedictorian, students could focus on finding value and enjoyment in developing skill and expertise in the subject.

Unfortunately, most often the switch to pass / fail systems does not alter the larger system-level incentives, leaving students to use pass / fail options as an opportunity to game the system. According to one 1972 review: "Students do not take pass-fail courses to explore areas outside of their own major, but rather do so in order to make things easier for themselves in terms of course work."[21] A study of a Canadian university that same year found that "students do fewer of the assigned readings and attend fewer classes in courses elected under pass-fail than they do with courses elected under the conventional grading system."[22] Likewise, a study of students at the University of Illinois found that they were working only hard enough to get a D, the lowest passing grade.[23]

Contract grading, or specification grading, is similar to pass / fail grading in its effort to dial back the importance of grades by reducing assessment to a binary. First developed in the 1920s by Helen Parkhurst at the Dalton School (and called "The Dalton Laboratory Plan"), the idea was that students would essentially agree to contracts around the work that would be done and the way that they would be evaluated.[24] The notion of a contract, nominally negotiated between teacher and student, was intended to embrace the spirit of progressive education's preference for "child-centered" learning by allowing the student to have some say in the direction and outcome of course assignments and the possibility of different outcomes for different students.

Since its introduction, contract grading has taken on many different forms in many different contexts, all with an eye toward empowering students around the aims of a course and reducing the focus on specific grade attainment.[25] During the 1970s, the idea achieved a small foothold in certain institutions of higher education. For instance, the College of Creative Studies at UC Santa Barbara adopted an evaluation system in which all students who completed all the work for a class received full credit.

More recently, a version of contract grading called "specifications grading" or "specs grading" has been popularized by sociologist Linda Nilson. As she explains in the introduction of her book on the subject, the motivation behind opting for a specifications grading system is that "it gives faculty strategies for developing and grading assessments that reduce time and stress, shift responsibility to students to earn grades rather than 'receive' them, reduce antagonism between evaluator and the evaluated, and increase student receptivity to feedback." And that is just the value on the instructor side. Specifications grading is also supposed to "enhance [students'] motivations to do well, lower their stress and confusion about academic expectations, strengthen their work ethic, and ensure greater rigor in the educational enterprise." The sum total of these efforts, according to Nilson, is that the system "may restore some credibility to grades by demonstrating how they can reflect the learning outcomes students achieve."[26]

One strength of the contract grading system is that it provides a great deal of flexibility for instructors. Depending on the course, instructors can decide to offer full or no credit for any given "spec." They can also articulate different levels of work as eligible for different grades (e.g., a 1500-word essay on three articles for an A; a 1000-word essay on two articles for a B), and they can determine how the various assignments in a course aggregate to final evaluation, whether pass / fail or for a letter grade. There is a danger, though, that spec grading devolves into a defensive, mechanistic process. In order to minimize the amount of time required for grading and to reduce antagonism around grading, instructors may emphasize the procedural, formal components rather than substantive elements of the learning process. That said, if reducing grades to procedural matters creates space to focus on the content of the assignment, the shift could be a net positive.

Food for Thought

Contract and pass / fail courses have the potential to increase the intrinsic motivation of students for learning. Though evidence suggests that grades and evaluation can be a strong and positive influence on student learning, motivation can easily slide toward stress and anxiety. Providing students with genuine opportunities to set the terms and goals of the assignments in open negotiation with their teachers provides them with the kind of agency and ownership over their education that many people would consider ideal; it is also good practice for learning and working in contexts beyond school. But contract grading depends a great deal on the instructors who implement it. If such a system is used in a strictly defensive way, to prevent instructors from having to invest the time to deliver feedback or from having to make difficult assessments about the quality of student work, then it is hard to see what has been gained in this shift. Students are likely to approach such classes in the same way they do now: by sizing up the path of least resistance to securing their desired grade. Also, if the opportunity to enter into a contract over the work in the course is less like a negotiation and more like a request to sign a terms of service agreement—if you want to use this product, then sign here—students may be less likely to feel intrinsically motivated.

In terms of the short- and long-haul value of the communication provided by pass / fail and contract grading, it's a mixed bag. The hope is that de-weaponizing grades will open up more opportunities for instructors to give substantive, lower-stakes feedback to students. But there is nothing inherent about pass / fail that ensures this will occur. The risk of eliminating meaningful information from the long-haul communication capacity of grades, on the other hand, is considerable. A transcript full of course evaluations that merely reads "P" from top to bottom leaves something to be desired. In the absence of additional detail, one is likely to rely on the reputation of the school itself—one reason why graduate programs, especially at elite universities, often have "high pass / pass / fail" grading systems. The limited value of P / F on a transcript is why many colleges will allow students to take courses P / F outside their major but limit the courses that can be taken P / F *within* the major. In the areas where it really counts, where students are likely to pursue jobs or graduate degrees, the extra detail of a letter grade is important.

For contract grading in particular, everything depends on how the contract grade is communicated. If a complicated series of contracts is reduced to a traditional grade, whether in the form of a letter or a pass / fail determination, it is hard to see what is gained from a communication standpoint. Likewise, if an extremely detailed contract is not summarized at all, it could provide a useful short-haul accounting of a student's work, though it would also create the kind of unwieldy long-haul communication challenge that hampers narrative grading systems.

To the extent that contract grading results in the kind of genuinely open negotiations that result in students in the same class pursuing substantive projects and developing different skills, then it poses a potentially difficult synchronization challenge. A grade on a transcript is unlikely to convey either the nature of the work performed in the course or the extent of the variation across students. Perhaps more expanded, detailed transcripts might try and incorporate some information about the contracts negotiated between teachers and students. This could provide more contextual information about the components of the grade, but only if future audiences know how to "read" and compare contracts across students. As with authentic assessments and portfolios, there is a deep tension between the potential open-ended features of the reform and the clear, reliable communication of transcripts we've come to expect from our schools.

Badge of Honor: Micro-Credentialing and Competency-Based Education

"Badging" or "micro-credentialing" has had something of a moment in the past decade. While portfolios have a whiff of the 1980s and 1990s about them, and reforms like narrative grading harken back to the 1960s and 1970s, badging feels new and inventive. Perhaps, as the latest alternative to the quantification of student learning, badging offers something that prior efforts have missed.

Or perhaps not.

At a conceptual level, badging is not materially different from what has long been called competency-based education (CBE). The premise of CBE is that traditional grades and course titles are too general and abstract to provide effective communication about what students know and can do. Rather than receive an overall grade in math or English, the class should be broken down into its constituent skills, and students should be evaluated on each individually.

In addition to emphasizing the specific skills or tasks that we want students to gain mastery in, proponents of CBE also argue that emphasizing and evaluating competency is better than traditional grading because it suggests a growth-oriented, developmental frame. It also, theoretically, allows students to progress at their own rate on each of the articulated skills. Students who have not yet gained competence or mastery of a skill can be encouraged to revise their work or continue to practice, while those who have already obtained mastery can move on to new competencies and new challenges. Advocates claim there is an important equity dimension to this approach to grading, arguing that when we fail to break a grade-level course down into its component skills, students can end up receiving passing grades despite not achieving competence in particular skills. Allowing a student to pass a class despite lacking competency in some areas, such advocates argue, ultimately does them a disservice.

Badging has brought a more modern touch to CBE by making it digital and by "gamifying" it—incorporating elements (e.g., points, tokens, power-ups) of video games. This digital gloss has gone a long way to reinvigorate CBE. Were that not the case, badging might seem somewhat ludicrous—like an extension of a Boy Scout's festooning of his uniforms and sashes. As digital products, however, these badges can be easily stored and shared. There is also the potential for schools to embed more information in the badge than would be possible with a patch-sized real-world object.

Badging also takes the traditional disaggregation of competencies and skills under CBE to the next level, by making a student's selection of badges extremely customizable. Especially in the context of online learning, where there are many available modules, students can assemble their own skill packages and chart their own journeys through the available curriculum. Yet here we encounter a challenge, because students often aren't sure what skills they actually need, and they don't always perceive their future needs correctly (just ask any student who took Latin because "it will be useful in medical school"). Even if students had a sense of relevant packages of skills, knowing what order they should be pursued in presents still another challenge. Ultimately, the student faces a crucial and difficult question: what is the body of knowledge and skills that defines understanding or expertise in a given field? The whole point of traditional curricular and degree requirements is to shift the burden of answering those questions from the student to experts in the field. But badging "empowers" students by shifting the burden back.

Now, however, we begin to see some of the limits to badging as an approach. Inherent to the idea is a reframing of each element of a class as an opportunity to gain points, credits, and tokens. Earn enough points and you get a badge. Earn enough badges and you can level up to a micro-credential. The idea is that accumulating and redeeming points, badges, and credentials is a *good thing*—a game structure that, by explicit design, aims to motivate students with these extrinsic rewards. Some proponents even discuss "gamification" of education as a "disruptive innovation"—promising that it can revive student interest in any subject, in any classroom, at any level of schooling.

Yet, as we know, credentials can usually be acquired without requisite learning. Many people already worry that students see the elements of learning as commodified—that they strategize about how to do the least amount of work in order to reap the maximum possible reward. Rather than shy away from this tendency, advocates of a gamification approach argue that we should embrace it—stoke students' competitive passions with leaderboards and point-based rewards. Though some gamification advocates argue that the games can be collaborative and need not pit students against one another, very little consideration or space is given over to student learning interests that cannot be decomposed into discrete tasks for reward or to student motivations that are not strictly instrumental. Whatever the learning task, the rules, rewards, and constructs of the gamified environment need to be placed at the center of the learning experience.

Beyond the micro considerations of the construction of the learning environment, there are also difficult considerations about the way badges or micro-credentials are presented to learners. The fact that many badging environments are strictly online should make us particularly cautious.

First, we should be concerned about the potential for decentralization. While decentralization can often be a good thing—allowing for local experimentation and innovation—it can also open a field to unqualified actors, particularly if it isn't carefully regulated. How do we feel about Arizona State University issuing micro-credentials for the kinds of topics often taught in colleges and universities? Probably pretty good. How do we feel about the National Education Association issuing micro-credentials for various teaching specialties, as they do? Again, probably fine. But what about National Geographic, which also offers educational badging? What about ABCmouse—a subscription-based digital education program, owned by Age of Learning, Inc., which offers educational programming for children ages two to eight? For-profit businesses have always circled around the edges of K-12 and higher education, but generally have provided services rather than direct credentialing. What will happen if the sharks are invited into the pool?

While potentially intriguing to parents who want their children to stand out from the crowd, the open-ended, choose-your-own-adventure quality to badging should also give us pause. Whereas we generally agree about what a macro-credential—a course grade, perhaps, or a diploma—signifies, there is no standard for badging or micro-credentialing. This creates even more potential for a gap between the symbol and what it is attempting to signify. This problem is compounded the more "micro" the competencies or skills that are being credentialed. In some instances, they might be more accurately described as nano-credentials. To take but one example, Relay Graduate School of Education—a "non-traditional" teacher training institution—recently offered a micro-credential in "Checking for Understanding Using Gestures."[27] How many hundreds or thousands of such badges would a competent teacher need?

Even if the badging and micro-credentialing space were occupied by only reputable providers, we still need to be aware of the fact that merely breaking a credential into smaller pieces does not ensure learning. The idea of mastery learning is inherent in badges, but it isn't necessarily the case that students will master knowledge and skills simply as a result of participating in a badging process. Many people have essentially participated in a badging exercise when they have sat through online driver's education courses after being issued a speeding ticket, or mandatory sexual harassment training via an hour-long digital program that requires participants to complete short multiple-choice quizzes at the end of each section. But did they actually learn anything? They almost certainly earned their badges.

Moreover, micro-credentialing embraces a view that runs counter to the critique that most people have of modern course curricula: that there are *too many*, rather than *too few*, discrete subjects (and skills). Most critics argue that our insistence on breaking up knowledge into silos and presenting them piecemeal to students is a lamentable part of the school curriculum, not one to be celebrated and expanded. Yes, competencies can be designed to cut across traditional subject matter. But there is no getting away from the basic premise that badging is about breaking subjects into their component parts, as opposed to trying to assess tasks and expertise more holistically, as in the case of authentic assessments.

Food for Thought

As a form of communication, competency-based education and its digital counterparts—badging and micro-credentialing—offer a mixed bag. Breaking down courses and providing information on the specific skills that students have and haven't mastered within a course can be a potentially useful way to communicate additional information to students and families. This is useful short-haul information. To the extent that, because they are digital, badges provide not just a fancy icon but also some evidence of work product, then they could potentially enhance long-haul communication as well. But there is a catch. In the same way that school reputation is often used to contextualize a student's grades, the reputational status of the schools, organizations, and private companies that offer microcredentials are likely going to be decisive in their value. Earning a badge in database management from Microsoft or Cisco is likely to mean a lot more than earning one from the guy down the street who hosts his website on a basement server. So curating, while maintaining some level of flexibility and choice, is key. Then again, one might reasonably ask whether Microsoft and Cisco should get to determine what schools teach.

Motivation is also a mixed bag when it comes to badging. Here there are two different kinds of concerns that require active management. The first is whether badging and gamification (the one does not necessarily require the other) create the kind of motivation that we want among students. There is certainly a reasonable danger that gamifying courses could dial up competition as students seek to collect more points, badges, and certifications than their classmates. The second is that while, in theory, a focus on mastery allows students to go at their own pace and to revise their work until they reach mastery, reality is more complicated.

The concept of students charting their own path and racing ahead of their peers also has significant equity implications. Reformers seeking to improve schools from the outside, and often projecting from their own experiences in school, tend to side with the precocious bright student who is held back and slowed down by the supposed lock-step pace of traditional classrooms. We certainly want all students to be challenged and to develop their skills to the fullest extent possible, but it is worth considering the issue from the other end of the achievement spectrum. The evidence on long-term student outcomes when students are asked to repeat courses or grade levels are mixed at best and detrimental at worst; and that is essentially what students will be asked to do under a strictly competency-based system.[28]

Getting to the Root of Multiple Problems

Concerns about our out-of-balance student assessment system have resulted in no shortage of reform ideas or small-scale experiments. Below, we return to the chart that we began the chapter with, only now with two new columns that reflect the ways in which the US-based reforms we examined in this chapter aim to address (but have not solved) the problems posed by grades, ratings, and rankings.

Many of the reforms have correctly identified and even been tailor-made to address a specific root cause. Unfortunately, however, the causes of present problems are multiple. Even when successful, these reforms have left some challenges unaddressed, and in other instances they have created new challenges that must be addressed by still other reforms.

They also share another common flaw: a failure to balance the system-level implications of their reforms. Because of how deeply embedded our assessment systems are in the structure, culture, and practice of schooling, a small change in one corner reverberates throughout the system. Though reformers would like those reverberations to lead to profound change, the system is more than capable of dampening the noise. Even more discouraging, having failed to disrupt the overall operation of the system, reform practice tends either to revert back toward the mean or become walled off completely.

Table 7.2

Current Problem	Root Cause	Alternative Approach	Remaining Challenge(s)
Gaming	Construct invalidity	Authentic assessment	Improving the validity of assessments does not change their stakes, which will still motivate students extrinsically. Moreover, their ability to send long-haul messages still depends on transcripts.
Weaponization	Permanence	Portfolio assessment	Assessing open-ended portfolio tasks in a psychometrically "reliable" fashion poses significant equity challenges. Their capacity for long-haul communication is uncertain.
Informational "thinness"	Compression	Narrative comments	Providing more detailed commentary on student work puts a heavy burden on instructors. Additionally, they require potentially problematic interpretation by future audiences.
Extrinsic motivation	Commodification	Pass / fail grading	Eliminating the motivation to pursue grades does not address the phenomenon of students putting in the minimal effort to "pass." Eliminating grades reduces the already limited information on transcripts even further.
Inequity	Manipulability	Competency-based education	Providing more opportunities to acquire competencies, or badges, could exacerbate gaming and the commodification of grades. It might also increase extrinsic motivation.

If we are going to succeed in reforming an assessment system that presently undermines student learning, we need to take a different approach. Rather than hoping that a change targeted at improving one component of the assessment system will work on its own, we need to take a more systematic, holistic review of reform. This is no doubt a more challenging approach, but it is also more likely to succeed.

8

Sustaining Learning

When Americans first started funding local schools with tax dollars, and requiring all children to attend, their ambitions for student learning were fairly modest. They wanted all young people to become functionally literate and basically numerate. These skills would open up opportunities for participation in public life and the growing market—enabling them to do more than simply work on the disappearing family farms that once shaped social and economic life. They also wanted young people from various walks of life to attend school commonly—to learn not just *with* each other, but also *from* each other.

As these basic aims were fulfilled, Americans continued to want more and more from their schools. They wanted students to learn higher-order skills and take a wider range of courses. They wanted them to be ready for jobs, as well as to be prepared for higher education. They wanted the schools to level the playing field—to begin fulfilling the obligations implied by the nation's high-minded rhetoric about freedom and equality of opportunity—while simultaneously sanctioning an elite selected on the basis of merit. All of this required new systems and structures for measuring and communicating about student learning.

For parents, tracking student progress firsthand had become more difficult. What did it mean to be at "grade-level"? And if students were increasingly competing against each other for distinction, how would academic achievement and aptitude be appraised? How might that be done in some reasonably fair way? In what manner would these achievements be recorded and shared?

As the system grew larger and more complex—serving more students, for more years of schooling, across a wider range of knowledge and skills—its bureaucratic requirements for information also expanded. Schools had once assured taxpayers of their quality simply by inviting them to observe. In small local communities, such face-to-face relationships were both possible and pragmatic. The state, having no involvement in the process beyond issuing a broad directive that local communities must fund their own schools and meet basic facility and curricular standards, largely resigned itself to record-keeping. But by the early twentieth century, students were moving beyond local grammar schools and attending high school at rates that would soon approach universal; some were even continuing on to higher education. All of this required some common currency—a standard set of tokens, and the shared language of numbers or symbols—that could be processed at scale. Growing bureaucracies required records, too, which enable such rule-based systems to operate.

In other parts of the world, the story was much the same. Small differences did characterize one country's approach from another's, but the pattern was generally similar. Why? Because the technologies used to track student learning in the United States were not works of art, produced through a process of creativity. Instead, they were simple tools developed in response to standard problems encountered by all societies trying to educate large numbers of children. How would students be motivated if they were compelled by law to attend school? How would parents track their children's progress if the curriculum were oriented around more than just the acquisition of basic skills? How would students be selected for various forms of further study if their opportunities were not to be identical? How would the most talented students be recognized, if scholastic aptitude were to become a sorting mechanism for social and economic advantages? How would the state monitor the enterprise of schooling so it could execute its fiduciary responsibilities and be accountable to the public? These are basic questions that most countries have faced as they have developed universal, tax-supported, public education systems.

Of course, much of the story of grades, test scores, and transcripts is also a *cultural* history, and not merely a technical one. Once a standard set of assessment technologies emerged, they became a part of the common experience in the United States. Because most Americans experienced grades, test scores, and transcripts as a central feature of their schooling experiences, they developed particular expectations about the functions of a "real" school.

Did grades motivate actual learning? In most cases, probably not. Did standardized test scores accurately capture their knowledge and skills? Hardly. Were transcripts a fair and truthful portrait of their academic careers? For most students, that would be a stretch. And yet most graduates would go on to support the use of these kinds of tools in their own children's schools, because they were markers of legitimacy. Schools give grades. Students sit for tests. Transcripts are the permanent academic record.

Once these practices became widespread, school leaders, teachers, and parents became invested in perpetuating this culture. These were the markers of legitimacy and success. And those who succeeded in the education system were even more likely to accept its basic features, as well as to ensure the perpetuation of the status quo. They erected structures—state accountability systems, college admissions procedures, and so on—that further entrenched a common set of technologies. The influence of American empire further ensured that these technologies were increasingly adopted elsewhere.

As a result, we have inherited not just a country, but in many cases also a *world* in which there is a standard approach to assessing student learning. Today, most of us live in a world of scores.

Within each class they take and across their school experiences, many students will strategize and carefully tailor their efforts, not to ensure they get the most out of their learning experiences or to develop their skills to the fullest—though this may happen along the way—but, instead, to get ahead and *stay* ahead of their peers. And it's hard to blame them. In a system where a few letters and several key numbers come to stand in for years of work, who could fault students for asking whether a particular bit of information is going to be on the test or which Advanced Placement class offers the best chance to pad one's grade point average?

Even for students who opt out of this hustle, the fact remains that grades and test scores are still the coin of the schooling realm. It is a testament to the diversity of American schools that there are pockets of students and teachers who resist or reject the prevailing emphasis on grading, rating, and ranking. But these stances are defined in opposition to the predominant practice. When the message communicated is that you need the right grades and top scores or you'll be left behind, it takes special resolve to stay motivated and press forward with one's own individualized view of learning.

But what can we do? As we explored in Chapter 7, there is no shortage of alternative ideas. Imagining ways to reform existing practice has never been the challenge. Yet even if we found a way to unilaterally outlaw tests or grades, it wouldn't solve the problem. Though the education system in the United States is loosely organized and governed, assessment practices are anything but. Switching to measured levels of competencies or to pass / fail record-keeping doesn't eliminate the competition among students or the huge consequences of getting ahead or falling behind. It also doesn't eliminate the reliance of future schools and employers on the information produced in those moments. We've built our society with schools at the center, so we shouldn't be surprised that so many different actors and institutions have come to use the information from educational assessments in their decision-making. Nor should we be surprised that students have, rightly, perceived the whole enterprise as extremely high stakes.

Herein lies the biggest challenge of fixing our current system: despite their considerable limitations, our current assessment technologies—grades, tests, transcripts—perform necessary work and do so with a ruthless efficiency. Any replacement must, therefore, perform the same work and serve the same functions or risk becoming functionally irrelevant. At the same time, any replacement must minimize the unintended consequences of current approaches, which, as should be clear by this point in the book, are multiple.

From our perspective, as historians who have studied the slow evolution of these assessment technologies in response to the demands placed on the education system, we think that any way forward with a reasonable prospect of success must begin with a careful account of the various functions served by these tools. Only then can we begin to disentangle their multiple and varied purposes and recalibrate their operation within our schools in a way that sustains learning.

The Uses of Grades, Ratings, and Rankings

Why do we measure and record student learning in the manner we do? This is an essential question to answer if we are going to design effective alternatives, because we need to continue to fulfill the basic functions served by our existing assessment technologies. Grades, test scores, and transcripts aren't merely institutional detritus left over from a bygone era. Nor are they merely a cultural inheritance. Despite their flaws, they continue to serve a purpose in classrooms, schools, and society. It is, therefore, worth reiterating these functions before we consider solutions.

Function 1: Communication

Anyone not in immediate contact with students and their work is reliant upon educators for information about what students know and can do. The core question is, how can we take what teachers know about their pupils and communicate it in some clear and interpretable way?

At the most basic level, assessment technologies like grades, tests, and transcripts carry information. Even to travel a short distance—from one teacher to another, say, or from a school to a parent—these tools create the basic language of our education system.

The most immediate audiences want rich information about students. Families want to know how their children are doing, so that they can encourage, coax, and intervene as necessary. Likewise, educators want to know how students are doing, so that they can prepare appropriate levels of support. And, of course, students themselves ought to know how they are doing so that they can adjust their levels of effort or help-seeking in response to feedback.

Whether on an individual assignment, a progress report, or an end-of-year report card, grades do a good job of ferrying these messages from teachers to students, their parents, and others in the school. Combined with the additional contextual information available to those close to the classroom, these short-haul messages contain critically valuable information.

Though succinct, grades serve their purpose because they become prompts for additional information seeking. Without too much work, a parent or student can easily learn the full story behind the grade. What does the C in history *mean*? Where is the student struggling and how can support be offered? In many cases, parents can and do seek more information outside the bounds of the formal assessment system. And educators do the same. Many teachers, for instance, will simply walk down the hall and ask their colleagues to explain the background on a student. However, relying on such additional information seeking is not ideal. The overworked teacher with limited prep periods doesn't have time to get the full story behind each of her future students' grades. The same is true of parents. Not all parents have time in the day to call a teacher during the lunch period; and not all parents' concerns are treated with equal attention.

If these were the only messages that needed to be carried, a number of alternative possibilities would present themselves as good options. But, of course, the symbols we use to convey information about student learning are also expected to travel a much longer distance: from one school to another, or from a school to an employer. We have called this long-haul communication in the book. In such cases, some external actor is essentially asking teachers and schools to vouch for a student. Based on the professional judgment of those who have worked directly with the young person in question, what can be said about his or her knowledge and skills?

Long-haul communication often requires, or even demands, less rich and detailed information. Auto insurance companies offering discounts to "good students" don't much care what, exactly, a particular student knows and can do. They have identified a statistical relationship between some composite rating of students and the likelihood of a crash, and they want the information kept as simple and portable as possible. Colleges and universities may *want* more information about students—after all, they generally request far more from students, including lengthy personal essays—than can be stored on traditional transcripts. Yet they also face time constraints, particularly in the case of highly selective universities where tens of thousands of applicants need to be evaluated; such institutions require the compression of information into something comparable, like a grade point average.

There are also cases in which long-haul communication would benefit from decompressed information about student knowledge and skill. Employers, for instance, rely on proxies for student learning—proxies like GPAs—that are assumed to indicate more than they often do about the skills possessed by graduates. Unlike teachers and parents, employers generally can't just walk down the hall or pick up the phone to initiate a conversation with those who possess firsthand knowledge.

In sum, we expect our grades, ratings, and rankings to communicate multiple messages to multiple audiences. They are expected to serve as both prompts for more information and the final word on a student's performance. We expect these messages to be succinct, stable, and meaningful. In other words, we expect them to communicate in multiple registers and at multiple distances, all at once.

Function 2: Motivation

Given the choice, many young people would rather be anywhere but school. Even the best schools—schools with positive cultures, and which offer opportunities for creative and unstructured engagement—ask students to do things that are hard or that they simply wouldn't choose to do on their own. Learning isn't easy, even when it feels rewarding. For evidence of that, we need only look at how few adults pick up a foreign language, learn to play an instrument, or take up a new intellectual interest. Free from being compelled to learn, adults tend to devote their nonworking hours to leisure.

But simply forcing students to attend school won't ensure they will learn. Learning is an active process that involves invisible work and considerable effort. A student can sit inside a classroom all day, facing the teacher with eyes open, and simply refuse to take part. In fact, because students are compelled by law to attend school, as well as by their families, such acts of resistance are admirable in a way. Students see an opportunity to reclaim their agency and, as every teacher has experienced at some point, occasionally seize it.

Grades, ratings, and rankings, in this context, have been used to spur effort. Actual motivation, of course, *can* be generated among students: that's part of what great teachers do in their classrooms.

But that's difficult work that can't be codified into a large-scale practice. It's easier to establish a system of extrinsic rewards, as has happened in schools across the United States and around the globe. Grades, particularly, have been used as a way of getting students to take school seriously. Those grades live on their transcripts, sometimes alongside test scores (like AP exam scores), and often in combination with test score reports (like SAT and ACT results). This was Horace Mann's original idea when he hoped that report cards would serve as an academic "ledger"—keeping track of investments, profits, and losses. Students are frequently reminded of, and regularly confronted with, their contents. And the overall message is eminently clear: the record will travel with students long beyond their school careers and they can expect to make it available for inspection upon request. Students might not always be motivated to learn, but the threat of lifetime sanction might at least convince them to perform the outward appearance of academic work.

Given these messages, students frequently respond by gaming their permanent records. Many, without question, are harmed by this approach, learning less than they otherwise might have. But at least some students actually do *more* work because of the assessment systems in place in our schools. In the absence of school environments that nurture an intrinsic love of learning, getting good grades and achieving recognition for these accomplishments—whether from their teachers, parents, friends, or future employers—is a powerful motivator. And we shouldn't pretend otherwise, even if many would prefer that the reason for staying up all night and working through the weekend was to *learn* the material and not merely to earn a grade.

Function 3: Synchronization

We often talk about the "education system" in the United States. Yet ours is actually something of an amalgamated *nonsystem*. Local school districts, of which there are approximately thirteen thousand, operate with significant autonomy as it relates to the choice of curriculum, modes of instruction, and determination of teacher qualifications. Elementary schools are generally connected to middle and high schools via school district and state board administrative oversight. But K-12 and higher education operate independently from each other. High schools and colleges within a state are often well aligned, and sometimes colleges can exert considerable influence on school curricula and course offerings through their admissions requirements. But this influence is not the same as formal control, and even in publicly funded state education systems, state legislatures grant considerable institutional autonomy to individual schools and to the system as a whole.

In an alternative universe, the fragmentation of American education would be addressed through centralized system building. Indeed, some advocate for just such an approach to address our education system's ills.[1] A standard curriculum, for instance, would link K-12 schools to each other more tightly. Public governance of higher education, similarly, would enable policy leaders to connect the work of K-12 schools with colleges and universities. And "end-of-pathway" schools—vocational programs, terminal degree programs, and the like—would establish strong links with relevant industries and professional fields.

That is not how the American system evolved. Instead of a system built according to a centralized plan, education in the United

States developed, at all levels, in response to localized and organic demand. Often, as in the case of the delineation between high schools and colleges, order was imposed only after the sector had come into being and not necessarily as a result of explicit government action. Whether it was the separation of high schools and colleges or the creation of a standardized college entrance examination by the College Board, the United States has taken such a permissive approach that key linkages in the system have often been provided by third parties. This preference for decentralized, market-based coordination continues. When it comes to linking postsecondary education to the labor market, the United States recognizes many independent accreditation agencies to certify schools, and takes an extremely permissive approach: any school recognized by any of the multiple national or regional accreditation agencies is eligible to accept student loan dollars backed by the federal government. Supporting student demand for degrees, the government assumes that the market will take care of the rest. If there is a demand for training or credentials, some institution, whether nonprofit or for-profit, will presumably fill the demand.

There are clearly benefits to this approach. The United States has developed the most diverse and expansive, and arguably the highest quality, system of higher education in the world. Likewise, the history of local control that gives communities a strong stake and voice in their schools has ensured a level of connection and commitment to local institutions that would be difficult to sustain if the Department of Education in Washington, DC, called all the shots. But in exchange for this flexibility, the United States is especially reliant on assessment technologies—grades, tests, and transcripts— to tether the components of the system to each other. They are what allow schools and other organizations to work together without actually changing their independent infrastructure. Students, for instance, can transfer from one elementary school to another, and their testing histories can follow them, allowing their new schools to appropriately place them in special education courses, if necessary, English-acquisition courses, if appropriate, or academically accelerated courses. Despite not being connected to high schools in any substantive way, most colleges and universities can appraise student "fit" by evaluating transcripts. Though the schools in the system remain diverse, we have accepted that for the most part we should accept the information contained on transcripts at face value: an A is an A. This is the simplifying compromise we must accept in order to allow the variegated system to persist.

School systems in other countries have a slightly different need for synchronization. While in the United States these technologies serve as the limited ties that bind our loosely coordinated system together, in many other countries the synchronization function served by assessment technologies constitutes critical system infrastructure. The tight coupling of courses, textbooks, grading systems, and national examinations make even small deviations difficult and potentially highly disruptive. The ranking judgments of college entrance examinations, for instance, are the overwhelming determinant of where, and sometimes what, a student studies in higher education. This means that any change to the examination or selection process is both higher stakes and higher impact. In contrast to the United States, where a holistic admission system allows for the presentation of multiple forms of information (e.g., GPAs, extracurricular activities, SAT scores) and variation in selection criteria (e.g., making the SAT optional) across autonomous institutions, in more centralized systems there is less slack, meaning changes will reverberate everywhere at once.

Whether a school system is loosely or tightly coordinated, the synchronization role of grades, tests, and transcripts must be recognized and tended to. These basic organizational arrangements are fundamental features kept in place by tradition, law, and cultural expectations, and therefore unlikely to change in the short term. One needs only to look at the recent history of efforts in the United States to bring more standardization and coherence to our system to see how remote this possibility remains. The Common Core State Standards sought voluntary cooperation from individual states to achieve the mutually beneficial ends of achieving higher and more uniform standards (and assessments), but that effort imploded before it ever got off the ground. And the passage of the Every Student Succeeds Act in 2015 sought to foster more choice and variation by states, not less. In short, education in the United States remains as much of a nonsystem as ever. Whatever else it means, the state of our nonsystem almost certainly suggests that we will continue to rely on data and other forms of symbolic language to foster connections.

Assessment That Sustains Learning: A Reform Proposal

Any new approach that is going to replace the way we currently assess student learning in the United States must address the three purposes listed above—communication, motivation, and synchronization. And if the new approach is going to be *better,* it will need to be better at *these things.* At the same time, it must reduce negative consequences, and do so without introducing new ones.

Our core proposal centers on disentangling these three purposes from each other. Why? Because effective tools serve particular aims. A flathead screwdriver, for instance, can double as a chisel, but it makes an awful hammer. Assuming that grades, tests, and transcripts can work together to simultaneously advance three vastly different purposes is a mistake. Our continued acceptance of them is a product of just how little we actually think about these assessment technologies as tools; we merely accept them as a part of the grammar of schooling.

Beyond merely separating the various aims ostensibly advanced by these tools, we also propose reforms that would strengthen each of these newly separate purposes. Our hope is that by separating and strengthening, we can also rebalance the system by reducing the burden on each constituent element. Below, we lay out the steps that would lead us toward a system that better sustains learning.

Step 1: Separate the aims of short-haul communication and long-haul communication

Fused together, these aims undermine each other. A message intended for a distant bureaucracy or a future employer needs to be a different kind of message than one intended for a student and her family. One requires *thin* information, whereas the other requires *thick* information. Separately, however, these aims might be pursued more effectively with more targeted tools.

Reclaiming Short-Haul Communication

In the system we envision, student achievement will be communicated via teacher feedback that will *not* be incorporated into a student's permanent record. By removing the threat that a grade will follow a student for the rest of her school career, grades will be de-weaponized.

This move incorporates the insights of narrative grading, but without the possibility that it gets converted into a GPA, and without the pretense that it will suitably serve the long-haul communication function that history suggests it can't. These focused messages from teachers to the immediate audience of students and their families will truly be pieces of communication, not motivation. An A will not be a reward, and an F will not be a punishment, because the communication will be ephemeral (not permanent). This doesn't mean that a student won't feel pride in an A or feel the sting of a lower grade. But it will remove the fear stemming from anxiety about what that grade will or won't mean in the future. Feedback that can be given without being permanently recorded will simply signify how a student should interpret written feedback—as a nudge toward fine-tuning, or a call for more basic understanding.

We would be naïve to think that tweaking recording practices, by themselves, will change grading culture. For too long, instructors have actively considered the demands of traditional grading and assessment systems in how they approach their teaching; so, in adjusting how we grade, teachers will likely want to reconsider some of their existing teaching practices. Indeed, we believe that these changes in our tools will work most effectively if they are accompanied by shifts in approach that take advantage of the new affordances they provide. For instance, the value of de-weaponizing grades is that it allows teachers and students to take on bigger and more challenging projects—ones that don't need to translate neatly into a letter grade and don't need a measurable outcome. Portfolios of student work or other project-based systems that allow for continual rounds of feedback are particularly well-synched to this kind of grading system.

Other shifts in practice would also ensure we make the most of opportunities provided by this change in short-haul communication.

For instance, providing more opportunities for teachers to engage in substantive discussions about expectations, progress, and trajectories of students would be beneficial for reducing the general reliance on simple grade and test score information (this, of course, is true whether a school adopts our proposed changes or not). The same is true with parental communication. The history of failed shifts in grading practices demonstrates time and again that communication with families is absolutely critical. Families need to know how students are doing in school and need to hear that they are on track or, if not, how they can get them to where they need to be. Providing teachers and parents with more opportunities to engage in these conversations would go a long way to ensuring the success of any shift.

These suggestions are just starting points, of course. But in thinking about each aspect of the assessment system, our advice would be to focus on the key functions served by short-haul communication and plan accordingly:

☐ Provide thick descriptions of student abilities.
☐ Foster communication between teacher and pupil about a student's development as a *learner.*
☐ Foster communication between teachers and other immediate audiences (e.g., parents, next year's teacher) about how to support the student as a learner.

Reimagining Long-Haul Communication

In the system we envision, student achievement will be communicated through a common set of performance-based tasks, which will be aligned with a common set of competencies. These tasks will take forms like science experiments, essays, creative writing, and demonstrations of mathematical thinking. The results of student efforts on these tasks need not be compressed into letter or number grades on transcripts, but instead will be accessible to future audiences via digital portfolios that students carry with them from one level of school to the next. This kind of innovation is already being undertaken by groups like the Mastery Transcript Consortium, and we imagine that as more districts take seriously the variety of longhaul communications they want to have with future schools and employers, and as they recognize the affordances of digital technology, we will see many more productive innovations in this vein.

To those who scoff at the idea that we can develop a system incorporating both grades and portfolios, we would point to places in our education system that have already embraced such practices. For instance, the AP Studio Art portfolio is a reasonable analogue of what we envision, as is the International Baccalaureate program. Schools will prepare students to complete "exemplars" over the course of a number of years, and their work will build toward mastery as evidenced in those exemplars. Ideally, this would also involve changes to the way we record student grades. But whatever final evaluation is recorded, it is important that the *work itself* be more readily available to future audiences—allowing interested parties to see evidence of what students know and can do. This results in the best of both worlds: the ability to see the prior school's assessment at a glance and the ability to dig deeper as desired.

We think an approach that focuses on larger projects minimizes the negative features of grading—gaming, extrinsic motivation, busywork, and so on—and maximizes the positive features. And to the extent that people are worried that teachers will teach to the test, we say: let them teach to *this* test. As we have argued, we are skeptical of claims that we can eliminate grades and assessments entirely. The best we can do is to bring tests and our overarching learning goals into closer alignment. Unlike prior, NCLB-era attempts to do this with multiple-choice tests, this effort has a more credible chance of success because it requires a fundamental rethinking about the products produced as part of the evaluation: not penciled-in Scantron bubbles, but substantive intellectual products. Moreover, these competencies will extend across the cognitive and affective domains, encompassing a broad set of skills and traits.

This approach also avoids the major pitfalls of many prior efforts to shift away from grades to competencies by trying to "gamify" learning or by atomizing skills into micro-credentials. Many such efforts are heavily reliant on standardized assessments to award points and make determinations about mastery. We think this is ultimately a mistake and prefer reforms that take us in the opposite direction, focusing on big projects, skills, and competencies, and relying on the expertise and judgment of teachers rather than replacing them.

In combination with digital portfolios, which we envision being interpreted through holistic human judgment, we support the reasonable use of standardized tests. Though we know this recommendation will not be popular with many, we believe that attempts to eliminate standardized testing entirely are simply not realistic, nor are they helpful for sustaining the pluralistic approach that has been a hallmark of American education since the beginning. The public has always demanded some ability to monitor schools and to compare performance within and across districts. Rather than eliminating standardized testing, then, we aim to minimize its most pernicious elements.

For schools, this means reducing, and possibly eliminating, the stakes associated with testing. By doing so, we would dramatically reduce the incentive for gaming, which would do a great deal to curtail phenomena like teaching to the test and endless practice-testing. Minimizing the gaming response among schools would also produce more accurate data, particularly if the system were redesigned to direct resources—rather than sanctions—to lower-performing schools. In addition to changing the stakes, it will be important to reduce the overall footprint of testing. If our aim is to understand how students at a school are performing, then in most instances we don't need every single student to take every single test item. Instead, a matrix-sampling approach, like the one used for the National Assessment of Educational Progress, would allow students to take smaller portions of the test—portions that would then be combined to produce a valid portrait of overall school performance. The sampling approach has the benefit of assessing a wider selection of the curriculum (because not every student is assessed on each item), while at the same time limiting the total time spent on testing.

For students, we firmly reject the highest-stakes use of tests that result in categorical outcomes, as in the case of so-called exit exams that students must pass in order to secure a high school diploma. Yet, even as we reject the use of a standardized test as the sole basis for a high-stakes decision, we recognize the fact that standardized assessments are likely to maintain a place in our education system and that any time students are assessed, distinctions are created. Thus, while we can seek to lower stakes, we are unlikely to eliminate them entirely. In light of that, we have two recommendations. First, we believe that it is better to opt for reporting results in terms of fewer, broader categories, rather than in the form of continuous "point" scales. For example, we would prefer to see standardized assessments reported in terms of high pass, pass, and no pass. This change would help eliminate the problem of false precision that comes with so much test score reporting. Students, teachers, and the public often make a great deal of small differences in scores that are more likely the product of measurement error or random statistical variation than true difference. While some information would be lost in reporting large categories instead of specific scores, we think this trade is a reasonable one. Second, we believe that students must have opportunities to retake tests. This is important not only for lowering the temperature on testing, but also for allowing students to demonstrate growth. Tests like the SAT have already moved in this direction.

As with the enabling practices for short-haul communication, our suggestions about long-haul communication are illustrative and intended to highlight the key functions served:

☐ Provide compressed accounts of student work that can be unpacked later as needed.

☐ Provide holistic statements about the quality of student learning.

☐ Lower the temperature on standardized tests by avoiding the false precision of percentile rankings and allowing on-demand retests.

Step 2: Rebalance Intrinsic and Extrinsic Motivation

In our imagined system, motivation will no longer be hybridized with communication. By releasing motivation from the daily practice of grading—the so-called permanent record—students will no longer be driven primarily by scores and grades; this will drastically reduce the problems of grade inflation and grade grubbing. Instead, if students are motivated by their assignments, it will be because they see the value of work products tied to actual competencies, over which they might plausibly exert some agency. This is not to say that we can instill an intrinsic valuing of learning simply by removing the extrinsic motivation of grades. That will depend on elements like teacher practice, school culture, and family support. But addressing extrinsic motivation at least opens the door for conversations about how to foster intrinsic motivation.

We recognize that of all our imagined reforms, this might take the longest and be the hardest to achieve in practice. Teachers, certainly, have tried in their own classrooms to encourage students to set aside thoughts about grades and focus on the work; yet it is not so easily achieved. Students have learned how to "do" school—to divine what the teacher wants, to determine what information will or won't be tested, and to calibrate effort accordingly.[2] The change will be just as challenging for teachers who are accustomed to using the threat of assessment as a motivating tool for their students and, sometimes, to compensate for a less than engaging pedagogical approach.

Pretending that this will not be a big lift for teachers and students is not helpful. But we do think such a shift is possible. And we believe that the more our schools put student motivation at the center of conversations about course goals, assignments, and pedagogy, the better. We think this shift only has a realistic chance of working if it is done in the context of the changes to stakes that we discuss above. Too often, adults talk about changing student motivations without thinking about the full range of incentives presently built into the system. This is not students refusing to appreciate learning for its own sake; it is students not being willing to try learning for its own sake while being heavily incentivized to engage in learning as a high-stakes, scores-based game.

The practices developed to motivate students in place of the current system of explicit or veiled threats about GPAs and permanent records would ideally involve:

☐ Emphasizing the *use*-value rather than the *credential*-value of assignments and assessments.
☐ Allowing for student agency and choice.
☐ Minimizing, to the degree possible, the use of carrots and sticks.
☐ Framing learning opportunities as opportunities for *growth,* directed toward longer-term goals.

Step 3: Pursue Change but Don't Wear Blinders

The most common stumbling block for efforts to reform our assessment of student learning is a lack of attention to the synchronization function of grading, rating, and ranking—a function that holds our otherwise disparate system together. As much as we might like to let every school and community go in its own direction, preserving the common linkages that allow the system to operate smoothly is key. If we do not do this by design, it will happen—as it has in the past with the SAT and the Carnegie unit—by necessity, as institutions work to address the problem.

In order to preserve synchronization across institutions and organizations, we envision common performance tasks serving as entrance requirements at each level of the system. In cases where students have not demonstrated the competencies associated with a particular level of work, they can be identified for additional support and subsequently mainstreamed along with their peers. To those who might object that this approach introduces too much discretion and subjective judgment, we would make two replies. First, the current system already involves such discretion, but papers over it with the formalism of standardized course titles and grading systems. For instance, people already wonder aloud about whether all versions of, say, Algebra 1 are created equal. Calling for common performance tasks will not eliminate this variability; indeed, quite to the contrary, it is likely to preserve it. But, unlike in the current system, the focus will shift from the current formalisms to what students can actually do. Second, a system that emphasizes common tasks will be more consistent with the standards that now guide our school systems. Those documents emphasize skills, tasks, and facts, not course titles and grades.

As with digital portfolios, examples of standards built around common tasks have already been developed and are currently in use. For instance, the New York Performance Standards Consortium uses a series of performance-based assessment tasks involving both written and oral work, which are then embedded across the curriculum—a research paper in history class, a lab write-up in science class, and so on. These student-produced works are combined with standardized state level assessments in much the same way as we recommend. In this case, students must pass the New York State Regents examination in English language arts in addition to any other specific requirements a consortium school might add. We offer this as an example of how this kind of reform can be designed and implemented, not as the last word on how to do it.

The more that districts and states tap into the creative energies of their educators and curriculum specialists, the more likely we are to improve on these early models. We can even imagine a scenario in which groups of districts or states decide to pool their collective resources to develop common tasks, though the degree to which they do so would be (as it is now) a matter of voluntary cooperation.

Those who admire what countries like Finland have been able to accomplish with their school system will note that those countries have national standards that suffuse the decisions made at each level of schooling. We doubt Americans will adopt anything like that any time in the near future. But at the very least, we can ensure that the standards we do have are carried forward into the key synchronization elements of our system.

The most challenging point of synchronization, college admissions, will remain contentious. We do not kid ourselves: these high-stakes decisions will remain high-stakes. However, it should be noted that a very small sector of the United States' higher education system receives a disproportionate amount of consideration in the design of our assessments. The vast majority of American postsecondary students enroll in institutions that are open access—institutions where all students who meet certain minimum requirements are accepted. For the minority of students competing for places at the highest rungs, applications already turn on subjective assessments of a wide range of things: extracurricular activities, letters of recommendation, and the like. What we refer to as long-haul communications— transcripts, AP scores, SAT scores—already serve as only the most *basic* qualifications for students seeking admission to the most elite schools. Students who meet the standards on these criteria are then evaluated more holistically. Our system would allow for the preservation of this basic approach—we suspect standardized assessments like the SAT and the ACT, or whatever new tests evolve to replace them, will remain a component of our college admissions system.

This is consistent with the practices of virtually all countries with selective university systems; in most cases, those tests are much more consequential than our own. Regardless of the degree to which these national assessments remain in place, we can make the entirety of the grading and ranking system more humane and more substantive.

To preserve the synchronization functions of our assessment system, a reformed system should:

☐ Provide common assessments at key transitions in the system.
☐ Mark progress in uniform terms.
☐ Provide a basis for measuring the progress of individual students.

Taking the Lead

As the above discussion should make clear, the task of disentangling the elements of our current system, refashioning them, and putting them back together in a more balanced manner will take plenty of work. It would, of course, be easier if we could have one national conversation, followed by a single large-scale planning session about how to carry this forward. But since that isn't going to happen, at least not in the United States, we content ourselves with laying out the key actors who might begin this work, as well as how they might get started.

1. Universities. For better or worse, one reality of the extremely competitive, high-stakes system of admissions in US higher education is that colleges and universities have a great deal of power. Historically, colleges and universities have been much more willing than state or national governments to come together to solve collective, sector-wide problems. Their institutional autonomy can be a powerful asset and might be used to get the ball rolling on reform. Situated at the "end" of the system, colleges and universities can initiate "backwards mapping" at the K–12 level by shifting their admissions criteria. Though not governed by an organizing body, colleges and universities might nevertheless coordinate to initiate a sweeping national reform. Because of their prestige and influence, institutions of higher education historically have been instrumental in bringing large-scale changes to the K–12 system. It is at least plausible, then, that either consortia of elite colleges and universities or state higher education systems could be the standard-bearers for this new system; that said, we acknowledge that the odds of this happening are low.

2. *States.* As the only "governing" body on this list, states have a unique power to legislate sweeping changes. Particularly if they were to establish consortia—as in the admittedly uninspiring examples of PARCC and SmarterBalanced—states could radically alter the K–12 system, which would also have an effect on higher education. There is nothing preventing state legislatures from taking steps to adjust current grading practices, alter requirements for teacher licensure, or articulate the criteria for key transitions within the school system. There is also nothing that prevents states from continuing to push the US Department of Education and Congress to allow for greater flexibility and novel approaches to fulfill federal annual testing requirements as some states did during the pandemic.[3] In the past, states have used their power in these areas to implement largely unhelpful obstacles, like high school exit examinations, to

regulate school transitions. Yet there is nothing that prevents them from putting that power to more productive ends. States could also direct their postsecondary systems—from their community colleges to their flagship research universities—to explore and implement these changes.

3. *Districts.* Even if states and universities were to do nothing, districts could adopt some of these approaches. In the absence of state-level support, the key, in our view, is to focus on creating ecosystems where these new practices can thrive. This will require particular care in addressing linkages across the system. What is the plan for when students move between schools or across levels? Districts might, for example, insulate K-8 schools from grades, tests, and transcripts. Grades K-8 have no interaction with colleges and universities; and because K-8 and 9-12 schools are generally under the administration of districts, each district could develop its own policies for linking their K-8 and 9-12 schools, as well as determining what a student needs to demonstrate in order to make a smooth transition. These adjustments, even if they occur on a small scale, could make a large difference in how students experience and feel about school.

4. *Schools/Teachers.* Finally, there are things that schools, and even individual teachers, can do on their own. Ideally, states and schools would move on this issue together, and in a meaningful way. Yet even in the absence of these kinds of sweeping changes, we think teachers can take the lead in trying to change the culture around assessment. Indeed, in many cases, our grading and testing practices are treated as required policy when they are really just tradition. Figuring out what is actually required by state and district policy

could be an important first step. Regardless of local policy, the biggest place where teachers can take the lead is in exploring ways to separate the long-haul and short-haul communication purposes of assessment. Teachers might develop classroom-based, non-standard grading systems and use those as tools for directing students to think about the substance of feedback rather than the transcript. Teachers could also be much more explicit with their classes about the skills and competencies they want students to achieve during the year. While such conversations are common among professional educators and in policy documents, they are often much less explicit for students in our classrooms. Such a conversation, if taken up by teachers around the country, might ultimately facilitate large-scale change. We won't be able to change the broader culture of assessment if we can't first change the culture of individual classrooms and schools.

Getting Started

One of the reasons we decided to write this book is because we wanted to help people understand how we came to assess and record student learning the way we do, as well as how we might do better in the future. In our experience, educators in the United States and around the globe are never short of creative, innovative ideas to meet the needs of students. And we suspect that, if empowered, educators would do the same in this instance. Thus, while we believe that providing a turnkey reform model would short-circuit the process of discussion and sense-making that is critical for securing buy-in and driving forward educational change, we also believe we can provide some starting points for educators and officials looking to get the ball rolling. What we offer in this section, then, are the concepts

Table 8.1

Current Problem	Root Cause	To Sustain Learning
Extrinsic motivation	Commodification	Focus on use-value
Weaponization	Permanence	Make it overwritable
Gaming	Construct invalidity	Emphasize performance
Informational "thinness"	Compression	Make it double-clickable
Inequity	Manipulatable	Embrace multiple measures

we think are key to reorienting our assessment practices around student learning. We describe the thinking behind each of these below, and we encourage readers to use them as starting points for reflecting on current approaches to quantifying student learning and considering how they might change.

1. *Focus on use-value.* Use-value is the counterpart to exchange-value. Badges and credentials are valuable, currently, because they can be traded for advantage. They function as a currency in the human capital market. Grades, test scores, and transcripts are not so different from money in that sense. The "rich" in this scenario—those with straight As, perfect SAT scores, and laudable transcripts—gain access to social and economic rewards that their peers may never acquire. Yet, as we have discussed throughout this book, grades, ratings, and rankings at best imperfectly capture student knowledge and skill; at worst, they barely do so at all. As a result, the focus on the exchange-value of education undermines the actual use-value.

Education is quite useful, even when it isn't immediately applicable to one's future employment. And here we should stress that when we talk about use-value we have an expansive view of the term. Sometimes "use" is taken to mean vocational—that is, useful for getting a job—but we mean something closer to "useful for living a good life." Being able to draw or paint, for instance, may not be a marketable skill for most people, but it might bring them a great deal of happiness. The same is true for learning anything that is presently graded or scored or otherwise commodified in our schools, colleges, and universities. Whatever one's precise definition of "use," we are quite sure that much of the busywork of school that emphasizes the collection of tokens would not apply. Our failure to emphasize just how valuable it is to know things and to be able to do things means that we are never fully motivating students. Our failure to frame schooling as an incredible gift—one that we give at no cost in this country, to all young people—means that we are perpetually threatening students, or offering them ancillary inducements, in our effort to get them to take advantage of their educational opportunities.[4]

This problem won't be easy to solve. But we can begin addressing it in our homes, classrooms, and schools. We believe that it is essential to begin thinking about what we ask students to do in our schools. Busywork—work intended primarily to keep students occupied, as well as to produce an easily gradable artifact of student "learning"—is very much a product of not thinking critically about what is *useful* to learn. Focusing on assignments that keep the big picture of learning in view for the student is an essential part of ensuring that students don't experience learning as disembodied, atomized lessons to drift through. Of course, not every assignment in a class can be a grand project. But starting with a catalog of all the tasks that students are required to complete in a year, in a given class, or across classes, is a good place to begin a conversation. Which elements of our schools emphasize education's use-value, and which merely assume that the purpose is ultimately about acquiring tokens for exchange?

2. *Make it overwritable.* There is perhaps no phrase that instills more unnecessary fear in students than "this will go on your permanent record." And there is perhaps no practice that does more harm to learners who develop in atypical or nonlinear fashion. If someone can ride a bike, the time it took them to attain that competency is almost entirely irrelevant. Their ability to ride down the street is in no way impaired by the fact that at some prior date they could not. This would ideally be our attitude with regard to all learning— successful present performance overwrites previous failures. Yet that is not our attitude or our approach in elementary, secondary, or postsecondary education. Instead, scores begin piling up at the beginning of the school year and sit unchangeable in the gradebook . . . forever.

Just because we can record information and find it useful for short-term decision-making doesn't mean we have to keep that information permanently. Test scores, once they enter official databases, cannot be expunged. Transcripts are indelible. Why? The simplest answer is tradition. But we needn't repeat past practices merely because we long have. Especially when we consider the consequences of this practice, which weaponizes assessment and incentivizes a wide range of behaviors and reactions often inimical to learning, the status quo seems downright medieval. Instead of permanent marks, we can imagine assessment systems that update constantly to reflect what students know and can do *today.* Can the person in question ride a bike *now?* If so, previous struggles are suddenly no longer relevant information—they are archival noise that should be scrubbed from the data.

The more we move toward the adoption of standards-based schoolwork with an emphasis on skills and competencies, the easier it becomes to think in terms of a system that records in a binary and overwritable way whether students have obtained certain benchmarks. Adoption of these practices would also turn down the temperature on the competition for grades. It is important to note that, as with all these steps, overwriting is not itself a panacea. It is easy to imagine a scenario in which a subset of very high achieving students come to view any grade lower than an A as a failure. As a result, the possibility of overwriting would result in even more obsession over grades. We already see this to a certain degree with SAT scores. Wealthier students are more likely than their peers to take the test multiple times—a practice encouraged by the College Board allowing students to send schools only their highest score (causing the scores to be functionally overwritten), and by policies at some colleges that allow students to combine their best subsection scores from across multiple test administrations into a new "super score." This underscores the need for thoughtful incorporation of overwriting policies and practices to ensure that they promote equity. Indeed, research suggests, for instance, that universalizing the practice of retaking the SAT would reduce racial and economic disparities in SAT scores and college enrollment.[5]

In addition to rethinking our policies and scoring practices, we must also commit to reorienting our assignments. Many assignments as currently designed and assigned in classrooms aren't *worth* redoing, except to secure a higher grade. And that itself is a core aspect of the problem, because we don't think cultivating a view that multiple rounds of revision in pursuit of an improved work product or enhanced skill is, itself, problematic. Indeed, it would accurately describe what mastery looks like for most people in most endeavors, whether professional or personal. The key is having assignments for which renewed effort produces more value for the student than a higher grade. Even so, we must say that we don't think everything can or should be overwritable and opportunities for revision have to end somewhere. Still, we should begin thinking in new ways about what it means to establish a fixed record of student learning.

3. *Emphasize performance.* If we are interested in understanding and conveying what students know and can do, then it is important to actually assess what students know and can do. That probably seems obvious. But, in fact, it's fairly revolutionary. Emphasizing performance, rather than many of the other factors that influence student grades, we might begin asking tough questions about practices that previously seemed normal. Why, for instance, do we grade homework? A compelling argument could be made that homework measures someone's ability to engage in drudgery without giving up—that it is a good marker of stick-to-it-iveness. Yet that isn't what most supporters of the practice would say. Instead, they would likely make an argument about incentivizing students to complete their assignments. Or they might not have an answer at all. We grade homework because we've always graded homework. But completing homework in pre-algebra or world literature doesn't indicate much about a student's mastery of mathematical concepts or ability to write an essay. It just indicates that she handed in the paperwork.

In order to address this problem, we need to think more carefully about how our grades, ratings, and rankings might be made more valid.[6] Valid measures make gaming nearly impossible. If the measure of a person's ability to ride a bike is a test where an individual gets on the bicycle and rides it, then he had better learn to ride the bike; there's no other way to pass. Educators can take action on this fact inside their classrooms, thinking more critically about what gets recorded in their gradebooks. But schools, districts, and states also have a role to play here. How should we determine when a student is "done" with a particular level of school? Should it be based on a set number of hours in his seat? Or should it be based on the mastery of particular knowledge and skills?

4. *Make it double-clickable.* At the highest level of abstraction, our grades, ratings, and rankings tell us almost nothing. They are reduced to symbols—letters and numbers that signify some level of competence—and they refer to general knowledge in broad areas. The SAT, for instance, purports to measure "Reading," "Writing and Language," and "Math," and the ACT adds the category "Science." This is almost entirely useless from an information standpoint. Students, families, and educators learn only something very general about an individual's knowledge and skills. Yet many audiences want exactly this sort of symbolic information because it is easy to process and understand at a single glance. Thus, there is a tension between the level of detail that a parent might want, on the one hand, and the level of detail (that is to say, *not very detailed at all*) that a future employer might want. To date, that hasn't been much of a tension. Information is compressed and symbolic, and as a result, students and their families learn little that they didn't already know. This informational thinness, in turn, reinforces the exchange-value of grades, tests, and transcripts. They are treated like bank accounts rather than as feedback mechanisms.

One way of addressing this problem would be to create two sets of ledgers—one, much like the current system, which remains largely abstract and symbolic, and another, which would be much more detailed. Many private schools, for instance, offer students grades and narrative reports. But a better approach would create a single system in which detailed information accordions down to something compressed. In turn, compressed information could be expanded to produce something richer and more informative. We call this "double-clickable" information, drawing on the analogy of computer-based files. When you look at a file icon on your computer, it conveys a certain amount of information—the name of the file, the file type, and the last time it was modified. Compressed information might be enough for certain purposes but clicking on it opens it and allows you to inspect its full contents.

There is no practical reason why we can't develop and expand systems that allow for more aspects of student grades to be double-clickable by interested parties. Currently, we occasionally compensate for the non-clickability of our information by asking students to submit writing samples or portfolios of their work in addition to transcripts. But there is no reason we couldn't do this as a part of our regular assessment practice. There are elements that would still need to be worked out. One important feature of traditional transcripts that would need to be preserved is the "chain-of-custody" of the information. When we look at a transcript, we have a sense of assurance that the grades that appear were entered by the original teacher and were maintained without corruption. In order to be valuable, any expanded transcripts would need to have similar assurances. We would want to know that the work was the student's own and was completed in the manner prescribed by the school. Though there are details that require attention, such an approach is definitely within the reach of schools and districts.

5. *Embrace multiple measures.* It might at first seem that the problem with our approach to assessment is the technologies we have at our disposal. If only we had something better than grades or test scores

or transcripts, then our problems might disappear. That isn't so. Consider the problems associated with micro-credentialing—a new technology that purports to be a breakthrough in how we measure student learning. More often than not, micro-credentialing atomizes learning into the smallest possible units, while amplifying the tendency to emphasize the exchange-value of education over its use-value. From our view, this is mostly counterproductive, feeding into the worst tendencies of our current system.

The problem, as we see it, isn't so much with our technologies as it is with how we use them. And one of the chief flaws is our overreliance on them. There is a tendency to treat our assessment technologies as zero-sum—new ones should replace their old counterparts. This tendency leads to the kind of monoculture that almost always undermines the goal of capturing the richness of learning. By reducing the number of methods and techniques that we use to assess student learning, we increase the competition around each one. For this reason, we actually view the recent move by many colleges to eliminate the inclusion of the SAT and ACT as part of the college application process with some trepidation. Though well-intended, these shifts simply place greater emphasis on the remaining elements of the application. Now, the competition for every one-tenth of a grade point is even more consequential than before, as is the need to have a good set of recommendations and a compelling personal statement. Good riddance to the SAT; but be prepared for some negative unintended consequences.

Our advice is to always err on the side of pluralism when it comes to the evaluation and presentation of student work. What are the various touchpoints that we could introduce, such that we can see students from all angles, recognizing their strengths and their weaknesses, and making it impossible for the most advantaged to simply manipulate systems? Among other things, this would require us doing more to try to measure student "upside," since there are many students out there who haven't yet realized their potential. Whatever the case, we would much prefer to offer a more complete, if still partial, picture and rely on the holistic judgment of admissions officers and employers than to rely on a small number of measures that lend themselves to the easy application of mechanical rules.

There is nothing that prevents individual schools and districts from committing to make decisions on the basis of more rather than less information. In all settings, we encourage educators and officials to think about creating multiple, ideally parallel, pathways to qualification—resisting a single qualifying test score or grade point average. By relying on more information rather than less, we increase the likelihood that our assessment systems will embody what we try to communicate to our students: learning is complex and multifaceted. Our assessment systems should be, too.

Conclusion

*L*et's start with the bad news. No one is coming to save us. No consultant is going to sweep through and fix things for a fee. No new technology—digital, online, or otherwise—is going to change the game. No one is going to wake up one morning and realize that the answer was staring us in the face all along.

The problems inherent in how we assess student learning in the United States and around the world are what Horst Rittel and Melvin Webber call "wicked problems"—problems defined by their complexity and interconnectedness.[1] Wicked problems are so entangled across sectors and institutions that there will never be a clear solution, or even an obvious approach. As our journey through the past and present of grading, rating, and ranking has made clear, this definitely describes our assessment challenges in education. It isn't as if we can simply say "let's stop grading student work" or "let's begin demanding better tests." Indeed, people have already tried that; it hasn't worked. Each ostensible solution merely introduces new problems, while also failing to address the underlying issues that shape and constrain student learning.

Now that we've sufficiently lowered expectations, let's move on to the even worse news: wicked problems often can't be solved. Yet just because a problem can't be solved doesn't mean we should ignore it. It means, instead, that we need to reorient ourselves away from trying to *solve* the problem and toward understanding and *managing* it.[2] Here, then, is the ray of sunshine breaking through the clouds: even such a modest approach might accomplish a great deal.

Imagine a world in which the stakeholders in education—students, families, educators, and the broader public—all challenge and adjust their assumptions and beliefs about grades, tests, and transcripts. What if we stopped pretending that grades are an accurate measure of what students know and can do, or that the pursuit of grades can take place without damaging learning? What if we gave up the belief that tests can measure intelligence, that they can be used alone for high-stakes decisions, or that they can be adequately "aligned" with learning aims? What if we simply admitted that the student record as we know it is a deeply flawed instrument that often harms the least advantaged?

In such a world, we might at least take down the temperature on our assessments. By dialing back our faith in these technologies, we can reduce the magnitude of their impact and the severity of their consequences. Moreover, we might create the space for human deliberation to enter the fray. A little latitude for discernment, in other words—some wiggle room—might act as a necessary corrective.

Knowledge, then, might be half the battle. It might be even more than half. To merely become more aware of our flawed assumptions and beliefs, more attuned to the inadequacies of our assessment technologies, and more sensitive to the deep damage that these tools so often do to student learning would be, frankly, a triumph. Parents and educators would be better able to support the young people they care so much about. And students would be better advocates for themselves and stewards of their own learning. We have seen this happen in the past. The IQ test, for instance, once dominated many facets of schooling in the United States and around the world, but it has been relegated to the part of specialized bit player. Our fate isn't sealed; we can evolve in our uses of these tools.

But let's be even more optimistic. What might we seek to accomplish in the form of concrete change? Broadly speaking we might think of two models for change: top-down approaches, led by those in positions of power, and bottom-up approaches led by educators, students, and families.

In the first model, leaders—whether in higher education, state departments of education, school districts, or other sectors of the education system—might work to create policies, issue guidance, and build capacity to sustain learning. For instance, a district or state could invest in the development of course- and grade-spanning projects that reorient students away from the exchange-value of their work and toward its intrinsic value. Alternatively, a committed district or state could invest in the digital infrastructure necessary to make transcripts double-clickable. Although grading, rating, and ranking may seem like a part of our DNA by now, rooted as they are in the past and in our culture of assessment, we also know that present practices are deeply problematic. Moreover, because current assessment technologies will be difficult to displace, it is essential that leaders take an active role in directing us toward a future in which learning is more squarely at the center of schooling.

In the other model—bottom-up reform—those most directly affected by our present assessment technologies might agitate for more local kinds of change. Organizing at the level of the school, educators, students, and families can push for both formal and informal shifts in practice. At the K-12 level, for instance, they might advocate for the use of multiple measures in any assessment of student ability that determines access to honors or AP classes. In higher education, activist stakeholders might push to make their course grades overwritable across the semester, ensuring that a slow start or a single unsuccessful performance doesn't haunt students who might very well end up mastering the course material.

These top-down and bottom-up approaches are, of course, not mutually exclusive. Major changes in the history of education have been initiated by educators and students, as well as by leaders in state and federal government. And the odds of success are far greater if those in positions of power are working to create space for, as well as lending support to, those actors who are most likely to understand the particular needs of local communities.

Regardless of the approach taken, our advice would be to focus reform efforts on identifying the particular aspects of our current assessment practices that disproportionately distort learning given their value as tools of communication, motivation, or synchronization. By focusing on specifics and remaining clear-eyed about the unavoidable trade-offs, reformers will greatly increase the likelihood of success while minimizing the risk of unintended negative consequences.

Of course, any effort to change how we measure student learning is going to be competing for resources and attention with other priorities and programs. It's a simple fact that every school and district, as well as every college or university, is already struggling to move various initiatives forward while continuing to attend to their core organizational work. Adding another ball into the mix, and insisting that they simply juggle faster, may do more harm than good. But we want to make the case that this work is as important as anything else they might be doing.

Grades, tests, and transcripts stand in the way of student learning. Though this was never the original intent—these tools were created to solve real and pressing problems for educators and school officials—it is the current reality. Grading, rating, and ranking now routinely overwhelm, and even subvert, the core purpose of schooling: learning. Instead of directing and spurring the development of student knowledge and skill, they have become ends in themselves. This has been true for so long that many of us don't even see that as a problem.

We allow the status quo to persist at our own peril. But this kind of change effort is too basic to be appealing to self-styled education reformers. And the core problems hardly stoke any regular public outrage, except at the margins. As a result, the ways we assess student learning remain in place year after year. Grades, ratings, and rankings are an unloved part of the landscape, but they are features we have learned to live with.

Yet why should we live with them?

As we close this book, we want to return to the early grades again—to the classrooms least affected by the quantification of student learning. Perhaps if we knew what we were missing, we might be more inspired to act. And there is a clear view of what we are missing inside the classrooms serving our youngest students.

On a bright Tuesday morning, Sharon Kennedy's students are working on projects about insects. They are going out into the playground, collecting as many bugs as they can find, and bringing them back into the classroom to draw and classify—by color, shape, number of legs, and how "icky" they are (the suggestion of a budding scientific thinker named Maya). Ms. Kennedy is an excellent teacher. But that isn't the point. Across the hall, Roxanne Porter is doing something much the same with her students: collecting bugs, drawing pictures, and having students write "just-so" stories about how they came to look and act the way they do. She, too, is an excellent teacher. Yet what separates them from their peers in older grades is not so much their skill as the context in which they work.

Their students aren't graded for what they do, and nothing ends up in a permanent record. They don't sit for standardized tests. They aren't building resumes.

When families need to know something, Ms. Kennedy picks up the phone and calls them. And when Ms. Porter wants to explain something to a student, she sits down with her in a quiet place and talks through the issue. Evaluations of student work don't take the form of letters or numbers. Instead, each teacher gathers together what a student has done and shows families where their children are demonstrating strengths and where there's still room for growth.

Inside each of these kindergarten classrooms, students are motivated (or not) by the inherent value of the learning task. Generally, they're enchanted with puzzles and problems, rejoicing in their ability to solve them. They are captivated by the unexplained and determined to piece together answers. They are driven to unlock the skills that will allow them further into the world of knowledge. And each day they do this all by their own choice. They jam on their shoes, strap on their backpacks, and walk to school—a place that most of them seem to love. A little after 8 a.m., they are lined up, all smiles and energy; they wave goodbye to their families and enter a domain that belongs to them.

It isn't that learning becomes less valuable over time, or that the feeling of knowing things becomes less powerful. And it isn't that teachers in later grades are less caring or less capable. Instead, the problem is that we begin to rely less on the core elements of successful instruction—the conjuring of relational trust, the summoning of meaning, the charms and spells of inquiry and play—and more on a set of systems and structures that aren't up to the task. This isn't to say that grades, ratings, and rankings are the only roadblocks. Improving on how we measure student learning will not suddenly clear the path of obstacles. Yet it may be the first big boulder we need to clear. Together, we can lift it.

Notes

Introduction

1. Juliet E. Isselbacher and Amanda Y. Su, "An All-A Semester? Students Advocate for New Grading Models After Coronavirus Prompts Remote Classes," *The Harvard Crimson,* March 19, 2020, https://www.thecrimson.com/article/2020/3/19/harvard-coronavirus-grading-system-petitions/.

2. See, for instance, Jack Schneider, "Pass-Fail Raises the Question: What's the Point of Grades?" *New York Times,* June 25, 2020, https://www.nytimes.com/2020/06/25/opinion/coronavirus-school-grades.html; "ODE Needs to Offer Letter Grade AND Pass/Incomplete Option to Public High School Students," Change.org, accessed January 12, 2022, https://www.change.org/p/oregon-department-of-education-oregon-needs-to-offer-letter-grade-and-pass-no-pass-option-to-public-high-school-students?source_location=topic_page&use_react=false; *Kawika Smith v. Regents of the University of California* (Case No. RG19046222).

3. Kwame Anthony Appiah, "Despite the Pandemic, My College is Allowing Grades. Isn't that Unfair?" *New York Times,* May 12, 2020, https://www.nytimes.com/2020/05/12/magazine/despite-the-pandemic-my-college-is-allowing-grades-isnt-that-unfair.html.

4. Daphna Bassok, Scott Latham, and Anna Rorem, "Is Kindergarten the New First Grade?" *AERA Open* 2, no. 1 (2016): 1–31.

Chapter 1. How Grades Fail

1. Richard M. Ryan and Edward L. Deci, "When Rewards Compete with Nature: The Undermining of Intrinsic Motivation and Self-Regulation," in *Intrinsic and Extrinsic Motivation,* ed. Carol Sansone and Judith M. Harackiewicz (San Diego: Academic Press, 2000), 13–54.

2. David Labaree, "Public Goods, Private Goods: The American Struggle over Educational Goals," *American Educational Research Journal* 34, no. 1 (1997): 55–56.

3. "ODE Needs to Offer Letter Grade AND Pass / Incomplete Option to Public High School Students," Change.org, accessed January 12, 2022, https://www.change.org/p/oregon-department-of-education-oregon -needs-to-offer-letter-grade-and-pass-no-pass-option-to-public-high -school-students?source_location=topic_page&use_react=false.

4. "ODE Needs to Offer Letter Grade AND Pass / Incomplete Option to Public High School Students."

5. Dana Goldstein, "Should the Virus Mean Straight A's for Everyone?" *New York Times,* May 1, 2020, https://www.nytimes.com/2020/04 /30/us/coronavirus-high-school-grades.html?referringSource =articleShare.

6. "ODE Needs to Offer Letter Grade AND Pass / Incomplete Option to Public High School Students."

7. The argument that what schools are really good at is producing "hustlers" not learners is a central argument in David Labaree, *Someone Has to Fail: The Zero-Sum Game of Public Schooling* (Cambridge, MA: Harvard University Press, 2012).

8. Adam Ruben, "Confessions of a Former Grade Grubber," *Science,* Sept. 19, 2018, https://www.sciencemag.org/careers/2018/09/confessions -former-grade-grubber#.

9. Ruben, "Confessions of a Former Grade Grubber."

10. Mark G. Simkin and Alexander McLeod, "Why Do College Students Cheat?" *Journal of Business Ethics* 94, no. 3 (2010): 441–453.

11. Donald McCabe, "Cheating: Why Students Do It and How We Can Help Them Stop," in *Guiding Students from Cheating and Plagiarism to Honesty and Integrity: Strategies for Change,* ed. Ann Lathrop and Kathleen Foss (Westport, CT: Libraries Unlimited, 2005), 237.

12. "Student Cheating Found to Increase," *Education Week,* December 9, 2008, https://www.edweek.org/ew/articles/2008/12/10/15report-b1.h28.html.

13. McCabe, "Cheating: Why Students Do It and How We Can Help Them Stop," 239.

14. Labaree, "Public Goods, Private Goods," 54.

15. Annette Lareau, *Unequal Childhoods: Class, Race, and Family Life, with an Update a Decade Later* (Chicago: University of Chicago Press, 2011).

16. Sean F. Reardon, "The Widening Academic Achievement Gap Between the Rich and the Poor: New Evidence and Possible Explanations," in *Whither Opportunity? Rising Inequality, Schools, and Children's Life Chances,* ed. Greg J. Duncan and Richard J. Murnane (New York: Russell Sage Foundation, 2011).

17. Mimi Bong and Einar M. Skaalvik, "Academic Self-Concept and Self-Efficacy: How Different Are They Really?" *Educational Psychology Review* 15, no. 1 (2003): 1–40.

18. Prudence L. Carter, *Keepin' it Real: School Success Beyond Black and White* (New York: Oxford University Press, 2005).

19. Office of Research Education Consumer Guide, "The Comer School Development Program" (Washington, DC: U.S. Department of Education, September, 1993).

20. Seth Gershenson, "End the 'Easy A': Tougher Grading Standards Set More Students up for Success," *Education Next* 20, no. 2, https://www.educationnext.org/end-easy-a-tougher-grading-standards-set-students-up-success/.

21. Information available at https://www.gradeinflation.com/.

22. Stuart Rojstaczer and Christopher Healy, "Where A is Ordinary: The Evolution of American College and University Grading, 1940–2009," *Teachers College Record* 114, no. 7 (2012): 1–23.

23. Seth Gershenson, *Grade Inflation in High Schools (2005–2016)* (Fordham Foundation, 2018), 6.

24. Talia Bar, Vrinda Kadiyali, and Asaf Zussman, "Grade Information and Grade Inflation: The Cornell Experiment," *Journal of Economic Perspectives* 23, no. 3 (2009): 93–108.

25. Alicia S. Modestino, Daniel Shoag, and Joshua Balance, "Downskilling: Changes in Employer Skill Requirements over the Business Cycle," *Labour Economics* 41 (2016): 333–347; for a historical perspective see David K. Brown, "The Social Sources of Educational Credentialism: Status Cultures, Labor Markets, and Organizations." *Sociology of Education* (2001): 19–34.

26. Peter Blair and Bobby Chung, "Occupational Licensing Reduces Racial and Gender Wage Gaps: Evidence from the Survey of Income and Program Participation," Working Paper 2017–50, Human Capital Economic Opportunity Working Group (2017), https://hceconomics .uchicago.edu/research/working-paper/occupational-licensing-reduces -racial-and-gender-wage-gaps-evidence-survey; Marc T. Law and Mindy S. Marks, "Effects of Occupational Licensing Laws on Minorities: Evidence from the Progressive Era," *The Journal of Law and Economics* 52, no. 2 (2009): 351–366.

27. Shannon McLoud, "I Get Paid for 180 Days of Work Each Year, But I Actually Work More Than 250," *We Are Teachers,* June 10, 2019, https://www.weareteachers.com/teacher-overtime/.

28. Gary Dohrer, "Do Teachers' Comments on Students' Papers Help?" *College Teaching* 39, no. 2 (1991): 48–54.

29. Beth R. Crisp, "Is It Worth the Effort? How Feedback Influences Students' Subsequent Submission of Assessable Work," *Assessment and Evaluation in Higher Education* 32, no. 5 (2007): 571–581.

30. It is worth noting that we do precisely the same thing with course titles. Given the decentralized organization of American schools and the lack of a uniform curriculum across districts, it would be entirely unfair if the UC system suddenly decided that some "Algebra I" classes weren't up to snuff. In reality, that may be *true;* but the fact that we pretend it isn't—that classes are classes and grades are grades—it allows the system to operate despite the decentralization and lack of uniformity in curriculum, textbooks, or other key aspects of instruction.

Chapter 2. This Is a Test

1. A lot has been written on the history of intelligence testing. Two of the best are Stephen Jay Gould, *The Mismeasure of Man* (New York: W. W. Norton, 1981); John Carson, *The Measure of Merit: Talents, Intelligence, and Inequality in the French and American Republics, 1750–1940* (Princeton, NJ: Princeton University Press, 2007).

2. Thurston Domina, Andrew McEachin, Paul Hanselman, Priyanka Agarwal, NaYoung Hwang, and Ryan W. Lewis, "Beyond Tracking and Detracking: The Dimensions of Organizational Differentiation in Schools," *Sociology of Education* 92, no. 3 (2019): 293–322.

3. Gould, *The Mismeasure of Man*, 34.

4. For a good history of the concerns around privacy and record-keeping that led to the creation of the Family Educational Rights and Privacy Act (FERPA), see Sarah Igo, *The Known Citizen: A History of Privacy in America* (Cambridge, MA: Harvard University Press, 2018): 221–263.

5. Jack Schneider, "Privilege, Equity, and the Advanced Placement Program: Tug of War," *Journal of Curriculum Studies* 41, no. 6 (2009): 813–831.

6. U.S. News & World Report, "2021 Best High School Rankings FAQs," https://www.usnews.com/education/best-high-schools/articles/rankings-faq#2.

7. College Board, "AP Program Results: Class of 2020," https://reports.collegeboard.org/ap-program-results.

8. Jack Schneider, *Beyond Test Scores: A Better Way to Measure School Quality* (Cambridge, MA: Harvard University Press, 2017).

9. Jack Schneider and Andrew Saultz, "Authority and Control: The Tension at the Heart of Standards-Based Accountability," *Harvard Educational Review* 90, no. 3 (2020): 419–445.

10. David Berliner, "Rational Responses to High Stakes Testing: The Case of Curriculum Narrowing and the Harm that Follows," *Cambridge Journal of Education* 41, no. 3 (2011): 287–302; Thomas S. Dee, Brian Jacob, and Nathaniel L. Schwartz, "The Effects of NCLB on School Resources and Practices," *Educational Evaluation and Policy Analysis* 35, no. 2 (2013): 252–279; Sarah J. McCarthey, "The Impact of No Child Left Behind on Teachers' Writing Instruction," *Written Communication* 25, no. 4 (2008): 462–505; Barnett Berry, "The Reauthorization of

No Child Left Behind: Views from the Nation's Best Teachers," (2007) http://www.nxtbook.com/nxtbooks/ctq/nclb/; Laura S. Hamilton, Brian M. Stecher, Julie A. Marsh, Jennifer Sloan McCombs, Abby Robyn, Jennifer Russell, Scott Naftel, and Heather Barney, *Standards-Based Accountability under No Child Left Behind: Experiences of Teachers and Administrators in Three States* (Santa Monica, CA: RAND, 2007); Margaret S. Crocco and Arthur T. Costigan, "The Narrowing of Curriculum and Pedagogy in the Age of Accountability: Urban Educators Speak Out," *Urban Education* 42, no. 6 (2007): 512–535; David Hursh, "Exacerbating Inequality: The Failed Promise of the No Child Left Behind Act," *Race Ethnicity and Education* 10, no. 3 (2007): 295–308.

11. Jennifer Booher-Jennings, "Below the Bubble: 'Educational Triage' and the Texas Accountability System," *American Educational Research Journal* 42, no. 2 (2005): 231–268; Jennifer Jennings and Heeju Sohn, "Measure for Measure: How Proficiency-Based Accountability Systems Affect Inequality in Academic Achievement," *Sociology of Education* 87, no. 2 (2014): 125–141; Richard J. Murnane and John P. Papay, "Teachers' Views on No Child Left Behind: Support for the Principles, Concerns about the Practices," *Journal of Economic Perspectives* 24, no. 3 (2010): 151–166.

12. Evan Riehl and Meredith Welch, "Accountability, Test Prep Incentives, and the Design of Math and English Exams" *Journal of Policy Analysis and Management* (forthcoming). Though the evidence here is suggestive, it is important to note that this is only a partial explanation for the recurring pattern of larger test score gains in math than reading because we find these patterns not only in the results of high-stakes tests but in low-stakes tests like NAEP as well.

13. Howard Nelson, *Testing More, Teaching Less* (Washington, DC: American Federation of Teachers, 2013), https://www.aft.org/sites /default/files/news/testingmore2013.pdf.

14. The National Council on Teacher Quality has been tracking the evolution of state teacher evaluation policies throughout this period. See https://www.nctq.org/pages/State-of-the-States-2019:-Teacher -and-Principal-Evaluation-Policy. Just prior to the passage of ESSA in 2015, forty-three states required objective measures of student achievement be used in teacher evaluations, including seventeen states

that student growth be the "preponderant criterion" in teacher evaluations, NCTQ, "State of the States 2015: Evaluating Teaching, Leading, and Learning," (2015), accessed February 4, 2022, https://www.nctq.org/dmsView/StateofStates2015.

15. Many hoped that the Biden administration would continue to grant blanket waivers on federal testing requirements in 2021 as the administration had in 2020 but the administration declined to do so. Andrew Ujifusa, "States Still Must Give Standardized Tests This Year, Biden Administration Announces," *Education Week,* February 22, 2021, https://www.edweek.org/teaching-learning/states-still-must-give -standardized-tests-this-year-biden-administration-announces/2021/02.

16. The Leadership Conference on Civil and Human Rights, "Civil Rights Groups: 'We Oppose Anti-Testing Efforts,'" press release, May 5, 2015, http://www.civilrights.org/press/2015/anti-testing -efforts.html.

17. Jason A. Grissom and Christopher Redding, "Discretion and Disproportionality: Explaining the Underrepresentation of High-Achieving Students of Color in Gifted Programs," *AERA Open* 2, no. 1 (2015): 1–25. It is difficult to read the growing literature on the value of having a same-race teacher on long-term student outcomes as being unrelated to teacher biases of different-race teachers: Seth Gershenson, Cassandra M. D. Hart, Joshua Hyman, Constance Lindsay, and Nicholas W. Papageorge, *The Long-Run Impacts of Same-Race Teachers.* No. w25254. (National Bureau of Economic Research, 2018).

18. A. J. Alvero, Sonia Giebel, Ben Gebre-Medhin, Anthony Lising Antonio, Mitchell L. Stevens, and Benjamin W. Domingue, "Essay Content and Style are Strongly Related to Household Income and SAT Scores: Evidence from 60,000 Undergraduate Applications," *Science Advances* 7, no. 42 (2021): 1–10.

Chapter 3. Your Permanent Record

1. Kendall Trammell and Chris Boyette, "Remember that New SAT 'Adversity Score'? That's No Longer Happening," *CNN,* August 27, 2019, https://www.cnn.com/2019/08/27/us/college-board-sat -adversity-score-trnd/index.html.

2. Committee of Ten Report, quoted in Marc A. VanOverbeke, *The Standardization of American Schooling: Linking Secondary and Higher Education, 1870–1910* (New York: Palgrave Macmillan, 2008), 132.

3. Norman Foerster, *The American State University, Its Relation to Democracy* (Chapel Hill: The University of North Carolina Press, 1937), 666.

4. Ethan Hutt, "Formalism over Function: Compulsion, Courts, and the Rise of Educational Formalism in America, 1870–1930," *Teachers College Record* 114, no. 1 (2012): 1–27; Tracy L. Steffes, *School, Society, and State: A New Education to Govern Modern America, 1890–1940* (Chicago: University of Chicago Press, 2012).

5. "Our Selection Process," Stanford University, Undergraduate Admission, last modified July 28, 2021, https://admission.stanford.edu/apply /selection/index.html.

6. Scott Jaschik, "Record Numbers Take Advanced Placement Courses," *Inside Higher Education,* February 21, 2018, https://www .insidehighered.com/quicktakes/2018/02/21/record-numbers-take -advanced-placement-courses.

7. Heather Mason Kiefer, "Teens Seek Academic Edge in AP Courses," *Gallup,* January 27, 2004, https://news.gallup.com/poll/10423/teens -seek-academic-edge-courses.aspx.

8. CollegeVine, "Is It Better to Get a B in an Honors / AP / IB Course or an A in a Regular Course?" https://blog.collegevine.com/is-it-better -to-get-a-b-in-an-apibhonors-course-or-an-a-in-a-regular-course/.

9. CollegeVine, "Is It Better to Get a B in an Honors / AP / IB Course or an A in a Regular Course?" https://blog.collegevine.com/is-it-better -to-get-a-b-in-an-apibhonors-course-or-an-a-in-a-regular-course/.

10. Princeton Review, "What High School Classes Do Colleges Look For?" https://www.princetonreview.com/college-advice/choosing -high-school-classes.

11. College Board, "Honors and AP Courses," https://professionals .collegeboard.org/guidance/prepare/honors-ap.

12. "Weighted Grades, Latin Honors and Decile Rank," Spokane Public Schools, accessed January 12, 2022, https://www.spokaneschools.org /Page/413.

13. Thurston Domina, Andrew McEachin, Andrew Penner, and Emily Penner, "Aiming High and Falling Short: California's Eighth-Grade

Algebra-for-All Effort," *Educational Evaluation and Policy Analysis* 37, no. 3 (2015), 292.

14. Phillips Academy Andover, Course of Study 2018–2019, accessed January 12, 2022, https://www.andover.edu/files/COS2018–2019.pdf.

15. Philip T. Bain, Loyde V. Hales, and Leonard P. Rand, "Does Pass-Fail Encourage Exploration?" *College and University* 47, Fall (1971): 17–18.

16. University Registrar, University of Massachusetts, "Latin Honors Information," accessed January 12, 2022, https://www.umass.edu /registrar/students/diploma-and-graduation/latin-honors-information.

17. Richard L. Miller, "Choosing a Minor: Why, What and When," in *Academic Advising: A Handbook for Advisors and Students Volume 1: Models, Students, Topics, and Issues,* ed. Richard L. Miller and Jessica G. Irons (Society for the Teaching of Psychology, 2014), 135. Retrieved from http://teachpsych.org/ebooks/academic-advising-2014-vol1.

18. Quoted in *A Turning Point in Higher Education; the Inaugural Address of Charles William Eliot as President of Harvard College,* October 19, 1869, with an introduction by Nathan M. Pusey (Cambridge, MA: Harvard University Press, 1869), http://name.umdl.umich.edu/AJL7593.0001 .001.

19. Phillip W. Payton, "Origins of the Terms 'Major' and 'Minor' in American Higher Education," *History of Education Quarterly* 1, no. 2 (1961): 57–63.

20. National Center for Education Statistics, "Bachelor's Degrees Conferred by Postsecondary Institutions, by Field of Study: Selected Years, 1970–71 through 2016–17," *Digest of Educational Statistics,* (Washington, DC: U.S. Department of Education, 2018), https://nces .ed.gov/programs/digest/d18/tables/dt18_322.10.asp.

21. David, F. Kim, Scott Markham, and Joseph D. Cangelosi, "Why Students Pursue the Business Degree: A Comparison of Business Majors across Universities," *Journal of Education for Business* 78, no. 1 (2002): 28–32.

22. Charles R. Foster, Jr., "The Modern Report Card," *Hygiea,* (June 1940): 569.

23. "What's All the Fuss about Report Cards?" *Kiplinger Magazine,* (November 1955): 39.

24. "What's All the Fuss about Report Cards?" *Kiplinger Magazine,* (November 1955): 41.

25. Donald Hoyt, "Competence as the Basis for Credit and Credentialing," in *Credentialing Educational Accomplishment. Report and Recommendations of the Task Force on Educational Credit and Credentials*, ed. Jerry W. Miller and Olive Mills (Washington, DC: American Council on Education, 1978), 154.

26. Sidney B. Simon and James A. Bellanca, *Degrading the Grading Myths: A Primer of Alternatives to Grades and Marks* (Washington, DC: Association for Supervision and Curriculum Development, 1976), 62.

27. Alverno College, "Results, Rather than Grades," accessed January 12, 2022, https://www.alverno.edu/Registrar-Online-Courses.

28. Alverno College, *Building a Community of Learners: A Community Guide and Student Handbook, 2017–2018*.

29. Matt Barnum, "Maine Went All-in on 'Proficiency-Based Learning'— Then Rolled It Back. What Does That Mean for the Rest of the Country?" *Chalkbeat,* October 18, 2018, https://www.chalkbeat.org /2018/10/18/21105950/maine-went-all-in-on-proficiency-based -learning-then-rolled-it-back-what-does-that-mean-for-the-rest.

30. Karen Shakman, Brandon Foster, Noman Khanani, Jill Marcus, and Josh Cox, "'In Theory It's a Good Idea': Understanding Implementation of Proficiency-Based Education in Maine" (PDF, Education Development Center, 2018), 44, https://edc.org/sites /default/files/uploads/Understanding%20implementation%20of%20 PBE%20in%20Maine_EDC%2020180917.pdf.

Chapter 4. Tools of Necessity

1. Joseph Kett, *Merit: The History of a Founding Ideal from the American Revolution to the Twenty-First Century* (Ithaca, NY: Cornell University Press, 2013), 86–87.

2. Edward Earl Gordon, *Centuries of Tutoring: A Perspective on Childhood Education* (PhD diss., Loyola University Chicago, 1988).

3. Mary Ann Mason, *From Father's Property to Children's Rights: The History of Child Custody in the United States* (New York: Columbia University Press, 1994).

4. Ezra Stiles, *The Literary Diary of Ezra Stiles: 1782–1795*, vol. 3 (New York: Charles Scribner's Sons, 1901), 154.

5. Peter Searby, "A History of the University of Cambridge," in *A History of the University of Cambridge,* ed. C. N. L. Brooke, vol. 3 (Cambridge: Cambridge University Press, 1997), 150–170.

6. Searby, "A History of the University of Cambridge," 95.

7. John Gascoigne, "Mathematics and Meritocracy: The Emergence of the Cambridge Mathematical Tripos," *Social Studies* 14 (1984): 556, 568.

8. Gascoigne, "Mathematics and Meritocracy," 559.

9. Kett, *Merit,* 22–23.

10. Kett, *Merit,* 83.

11. Harvard University, *Annual Reports of the President and Treasurer of Harvard College, 1878–79* (Cambridge, MA: Harvard University, 1879), 9, 73.

12. Michael Moffatt, "Inventing the 'Time-Honored Traditions' of 'Old Rutgers': Rutgers Student Culture, 1858–1900," *The Journal of the Rutgers University Libraries* 47, no. 1 (1985): 4.

13. Andrew P. Peabody, *Harvard Reminiscences* (Boston: Ticknor, 1888).

14. William and Mary College, *Book of the Proceedings of the Society of William and Mary College* (Williamsburg, VA: William and Mary College, 1817), 15.

15. See, for instance, Jason M. Opal, "Exciting Emulation: Academies and the Transformation of the Rural North, 1780s–1820s," *Journal of American History* 91, no. 2 (2004): 445–470.

16. David F. Labaree, *The Making of an American High School: The Credentials Market and the Central High School of Philadelphia, 1838–1939* (New Haven, CT: Yale University Press, 1988).

17. Gideon F. Thayer, "Letters to a Young Teacher," *American Journal of Education* 2 (1856), 391–398.

18. Rita Koganzon, "'Producing a Reconciliation of Disinterestedness and Commerce': The Political Rhetoric of Education in the Early Republic," *History of Education Quarterly* 52, no. 3 (2012): 403–429; J. M. Opal, "Exciting Emulation: Academies and the Transformation of the Rural North, 1780s–1820s," *The Journal of American History* 91, no. 2 (2004): 445–470.

19. Harvard University, *Annual Report of the President of Harvard University to the Overseers on the State of the University for the Academic Year 1830–1831* (Cambridge, MA: Harvard University, 1831), 285.

20. Horace Mann, *Ninth Annual Report* (Boston: Dutton and Wentworth, State Printer, 1846), 504.

21. Mann, *Ninth Annual Report,* 508.

22. *The Connecticut Common School Journal and Annals of Education* 9, no. 12 (December 1862), 389.

23. On the role of exhibitions as a way of communicating with the public about the progress of students in schools, see William J. Reese, *Testing Wars in the Public Schools: A Forgotten History* (Cambridge, MA: Harvard University Press, 2013), 8–37.

24. "Intelligence," *Massachusetts Teacher* 28, no. 6 (June 1874), 258.

25. Ethan Hutt, "The State's Spectacles: Education Statistics, Representations of Schooling, and the Federal Government's Educational Sight," in *Production, Presentation, and Acceleration of Educational Research: Could Less Be More?,* ed. Paul Smeyers and Marc Depaepe (New York: Springer, 2021).

26. For a full length account of this history see Reese, *Testing Wars.*

27. Reese, *Testing Wars.*

28. Horace Mann, quoted in Reese, *Testing Wars,* 143.

29. Carter Alexander, *School Statistics and Publicity* (Boston: Silver, Burdett, 1919), 52–53.

30. K. T. Waugh, "A New Mental Diagnosis of the College Student," *New York Times,* January 2, 1916, SM12.

31. D. L. Geyer, *Introduction to the Use of Standardized Tests* (Chicago: Plymouth Press, 1922), 8.

32. Arthur L. Campbell, "Keeping the Score," *The School Review* 29, no. 7 (1921), 511.

33. E. J. Ashbaugh and H. B. Chapman, "Report Cards in American Cities," *Educational Research Bulletin* 4, no. 14 (1925): 291.

34. Leroy D. Weld, "A Standard of Interpretation of Numerical Grades," *The School Review* 25, no. 6 (1917): 412–421.

35. Ethan Hutt, "A Brief History of the Student Record," *Ithaka S+R* (2016), https://doi.org/10.18665/sr.283886.

36. The most famous treatise about the problem of overaged children and how they might be evidence of poorly administered schools is

undoubtedly Leonard Porter Ayres, *Laggards in Our Schools: A Study of Retardation and Elimination in City School Systems* (New York: Charities Publications Committe, 1909).

37. Campbell, "Keeping the Score," 511.

38. Max Meyer, "Experiences with the Grading System of the University of Missouri," *Science* 33, no. 852 (1911), 661.

39. Isador E. Finkelstein, *The Marking System in Theory and Practice* (Baltimore: Warwick and York, 1913), 11.

40. Finkelstein, *The Marking System in Theory and Practice*, 18.

41. Norman E. Rutt, "Grades and Distributions," *National Mathematics Magazine* 18, no. 3 (1943): 124.

42. Thorsten Veblen, *The Higher Learning in America: A Memorandum on the Conduct of Universities by Business Men* (New York: B. W. Huebsch, 1918), 128.

43. David Segel, "To Mark or Not to Mark, an Unsolved Problem," *School Life* 22, no. 2 (1936): 34.

44. R. G. Sumner, "What Price Marks?" *Junior-Senior High School Clearing House* 9, no. 6 (1935): 340.

45. G. H. Geyer, "Westwood High Goes off the 'Gold-Standard' Marking System," *The Clearing House* 12, no. 9 (1938): 531.

46. V. L. Beggs, "Reporting Pupil Progress Without Report Cards," *The Elementary School Journal* 37, no. 2 (1936): 107.

47. Millard E. Gladfelter, "Status and Trends of College-Entrance Requirements," *The School Review* 45, no. 10 (1937): 742.

48. David Tyack and Michael Berkowitz, "The Man Nobody Liked: Toward a Social History of the Truant Officer, 1840–1940," *American Quarterly* 29, no. 1 (1977): 31–54; Hutt, "A Brief History of the Student Record."

49. Arch Oliver Heck, *A Study of Child-Accounting Records* (Columbus: Ohio State University, 1925), 114.

50. George Drayton Strayer and Nickolaus Louis Englehardt, *A Score Card and Standards for the Records and Reports of City School Systems* (New York: Teachers College Press, 1923).

51. Ellen Condliffe Lagemann, *Private Power for the Public Good: A History of the Carnegie Foundation for the Advancement of Teaching* (Middletown,

CT: Wesleyan University Press, 1983); Marc A. VanOverbeke, *The Standardization of American Schooling: Linking Secondary and Higher Education, 1870–1910* (New York: Palgrave Macmillan, 2008).

52. For an excellent overview of this history, see VanOverbeke, *The Standardization of American Schooling*. See also Robert J. Gough, "High School Inspection by the University of Wisconsin, 1877–1931," *History of Education Quarterly* 50, no. 3 (2010): 263–297; David K. Brown, *Degrees of Control* (New York: Teachers College Press, 1995), 118–119.

53. P. P. Claxton, "Army Psychologists for City Public School Work," *School and Society* 9 (1919): 203–204.

54. Carter Alexander, "Presenting Educational Measurements So as to Influence the Public Favorably," *The Journal of Educational Research* 3, no. 5 (1921): 347–348.

55. F. J. Kelly, "The Kansas Silent Reading Test," *The Journal of Educational Psychology* 7, no. 2 (Feb. 1916): 63.

56. The best account of the history of early history of the Educational Testing Service and the SAT remains Nicholas Lemann, *The Big Test: The Secret History of the American Meritocracy* (New York: Farrar, Straus, Giroux, 1999). See also Michael Schudson, "Organizing the 'Meritocracy': A History of the College Entrance Examination Board," *Harvard Educational Review* 42, no. 1 (1972): 34–69.

57. Ethan Hutt, "The GED and the Rise of Contextless Accountability," *Teachers College Record* 116, no. 9 (2014): 1–20.

58. On the trend toward viewing school performance in national terms, see Ethan L. Hutt, "'Seeing like a State' in the Postwar Era: The Coleman Report, Longitudinal Datasets, and the Measurement of Human Capital," *History of Education Quarterly* 57, no. 4 (2017): 615–625.

59. Despite its prominence in media coverage and policy circles, we still lack a high-quality history of NAEP and its influence. For an overview of its origins and evolution, see Maris Vinovskis, *Overseeing the Nation's Report Card: The Creation and Evolution of the National Assessment Governing Board (NAGB)* (Washington, DC: National Assessment Governing Board, 2001); Lyle V. Jones, "A History of the National Assessment of Educational Progress and Some Questions about its Future," *Educational Researcher* 25, no. 7 (1996): 15–22.

Chapter 5. The Culture of Assessment

1. Michael Capuano, "With Test Resistance Rising Nationwide, What's Next for Federal Education Policy?" Citizens for Public Schools forum, Tufts University, Medford, MA, October 6, 2014.

2. Letter to parents from Redwood Day School (n.d.), author records.

3. Mary Metz, "Real School: A Universal Drama amid Disparate Experience," *Journal of Education Policy* 4, no. 5 (1989): 75–91; David Tyack and Larry Cuban, *Tinkering Toward Utopia: A Century of Public School Reform* (Cambridge, MA: Harvard University Press, 1995).

4. Dan Lortie, *Schoolteacher: A Sociological Study* (Chicago: University of Chicago Press, 1975); Larry Cuban, *How Teachers Taught: Constancy and Change in American Classrooms, 1890–1990* (New York: Teachers College Press, 1993).

5. Lortie, *Schoolteacher.*

6. Cassandra M. Guarino, Lucrecia Santibañez, and Glenn A. Daley, "Teacher Recruitment and Retention: A Review of the Recent Empirical Literature," *Review of Educational Research* 76, no. 2 (2006): 173–208.

7. The introduction of the Common Core State Standards was a particularly generative period for this genre of social media post. Two of the most widely shared involved a tweet by comedian Louis C. K. and a Facebook post in which an allegedly "frustrated parent" with a BS in electronics engineering completes his child's homework assignment to write a letter explaining how to derive the answer to a math problem by explaining why the traditional way of solving the problem using the subtraction algorithm not the number line is simpler and faster than the alternative proposed by the new curriculum. See Diane Ravitch, "Louis C. K. Takes Aim at Common Core—and We're All Smarter for It," *Huffpost,* July 2, 2014, https://www.huffpost.com/entry/louis-ck-common-core_b_5250982; The Patriot Post, *Facebook,* March 21, 2014, https://www.facebook.com/PatriotPost/photos/a.82108390913.80726.51560645913/10152143072400914/?type=1&stream_ref=10.

8. Adam Laats, *Fundamentalism and Education in the Scopes Era: God, Darwin, and the Roots of America's Culture Wars* (New York: Springer,

2010); Jonathan Zimmerman, *Whose America?: Culture Wars in the Public Schools* (Cambridge, MA: Harvard University Press, 2005); Jonathan Zimmerman, *Too Hot to Handle* (Princeton, NJ: Princeton University Press, 2015).

9. HS Grading for All, "ODE Needs to Offer Letter Grade AND Pass / Incomplete Option to Public High School Students," accessed January 10, 2022, https://www.change.org/p/oregon-department-of -education-oregon-needs-to-offer-letter-grade-and-pass-no-pass -option-to-public-high-school-students?source_location=topic _page&use_react=false.

10. Doug Shapiro, Afet Dundar, Phoebe Khasiala Wakhungu, Xin Yuan, Angel Nathan, and Yongsik Hwang, *Completing College: A National View of Student Attainment Rates—Fall 2010 Cohort* (Signature Report No. 12) (Herndon, VA: National Student Clearinghouse, 2016).

11. Prudence L. Carter, "Straddling Boundaries: Identity, Culture, and School." *Sociology of Education* 79, no. 4 (2006): 304–328; Miguel Ceja, "Understanding the Role of Parents and Siblings as Information Sources in the College Choice Process of Chicana Students," *Journal of College Student Development* 47, no. 1 (2006): 87–104; Michelle G., Knight, Nadjwa E.L. Norton, Courtney C. Bentley, and Iris R. Dixon, "The Power of Black and Latina / o Counterstories: Urban Families and College-Going Processes," *Anthropology & Education Quarterly* 35, no. 1 (2004): 99–120; A'Lesia Land, Jason R. Mixon, Jennifer Butcher, and Sandra Harris, "Stories of Six Successful African American Males High School Students: A Qualitative Study," *NASSP Bulletin* 98, no. 2 (June 2014): 142–162.

12. Matt Barnum, "Maine Went All In on 'Proficiency-Based Learning'— then Rolled it Back. What Does that Mean for the Rest of the Country?" *ChalkBeat,* October 18, 2018, https://www.chalkbeat.org/2018/10/18 /21105950/maine-went-all-in-on-proficiency-based-learning-then -rolled-it-back-what-does-that-mean-for-the-rest; Susan Cover, "Frustrated Maine Parents Rally Against Proficiency-Based Learning," *The Maine Monitor,* April 6, 2018, https://www.themainemonitor.org /frustrated-maine-parents-rally-against-proficiency-based-learning/; Kelly Field and Robbie Feinberg, "Inside Maine's Disastrous Rollout of Proficiency-Based Learning," *The Hechinger Report,* April 19, 2019,

https://hechingerreport.org/inside-maines-disastrous-roll-out-of
-proficiency-based-learning/.

13. Talia Bar, Vrinda Kadiyali, and Asaf Zussman, "Grade Information and Grade Inflation: The Cornell Experiment," *Journal of Economic Perspectives* 23, no. 3 (2009): 93–108.

14. Sorathan Chaturapruek, Thomas S. Dee, Ramesh Joahri, Rene F. Kizilcec, and Mitchell L. Stevens, "How a Data-Driven Course Planning Tool Affects College Students' GPA: Evidence from Two Field Experiments," *Proceedings of the Fifth Annual ACM Conference on Learning at Scale* (2018): 1–10.

15. Melissa Lazarin, *Testing Overload in America's Schools* (Washington, DC: Center for American Progress, 2014).

16. Ethan L. Hutt and Mitchell L. Stevens, "From Soldiers to Students: The Tests of General Educational Development (GED) as Diplomatic Measurement," *Social Science History* 41, no. 4 (2017): 731–755.

17. Mark Hlavacik and Jack Schneider, "The Echo of Reform Rhetoric: Arguments about National and Local School Failure in the News, 1984–2016," *American Journal of Education* 127, no. 4 (2021): 627–655.

18. The phrase, which has now been applied to many aspects of the American state, is from Elisabeth S. Clemens, "Lineages of the Rube Goldberg State: Building and Blurring Public Programs, 1900–1940," in *Rethinking Political Institutions: The Art of the State,* ed. Ian Shapiro, Stephen Skowronek, and Daniel Galvin (New York: New York University Press, 2006), 380–443.

19. Theodore M. Porter, *Trust in Numbers: The Pursuit of Objectivity in Science and Public Life* (Princeton, NJ: Princeton University Press, 1995).

20. James C. Scott, *Seeing Like a State* (New Haven, CT: Yale University Press, 1998).

21. This observation about the characteristics of numbers is indebted to Bruno Latour, *Science in Action: How to Follow Scientists and Engineers through Society* (Cambridge, MA: Harvard University Press, 1987); see also Michael Power, "Counting, Control, and Calculation: Reflections on Measuring Management," *Human Relations* 57, no. 6 (2004): 765–783.

22. Jack Schneider, *Beyond Test Scores: A Better Way to Measure School Quality* (Cambridge, MA: Harvard University Press, 2017).

23. Jack Schneider and Derek Gottlieb, "In Praise of Ordinary Measures: The Present Limits and Future Possibilities of Educational Accountability," *Educational Theory* 71, no. 4 (2021): 455–473; Derek Gottlieb and Jack Schneider, "Putting the Public Back into Public Accountability," *Phi Delta Kappan* 100, no. 3 (2018): 29–32.

24. Lawrence Cremin, *The Republic and the School: Horace Mann on the Education of Free Men* (New York: Teachers College Press, 1957).

25. Joseph F. Kett, *Merit: The History of a Founding Ideal from the American Revolution to the Twenty-First Century* (Ithaca, NY: Cornell University Press, 2012); James Bryant Conant, *Thomas Jefferson and the Development of American Public Education* (Berkeley: University of California Press, 1962).

26. David Labaree, *Someone Has to Fail: The Zero-Sum Game of Public Schooling* (Cambridge, MA: Harvard University Press, 2012).

27. Carolyn Sattin-Bajaj and Allison Roda, "Opportunity Hoarding in School Choice Contexts: The Role of Policy Design in Promoting Middle-Class Parents' Exclusionary Behaviors," *Educational Policy* 34, no. 7 (2020).

28. Herbert J. Walberg and Shiow-Ling Tsai, "Matthew Effects in Education," *American Educational Research Journal* 20, no. 3 (1983): 359–373.

Chapter 6. It's a Small World after All

1. European Centre for International Political Economy, "New Globalization," accessed January 11, 2022, https://ecipe.org/new -globalization/.

2. Ade Fajana, "Colonial Control and Education: The Development of Higher Education in Nigeria 1900–1950," *Journal of the Historical Society of Nigeria* 6, no. 3 (1972): 323.

3. Fajana, "Colonial Control and Education," 329.

4. Mary Haywood Metz, "Real School: A Universal Drama amid Disparate Experience," *Politics of Education Association Yearbook* 4, no. 5 (1989): 75–91.

5. Mathew B. Gwanfogbe, *Changing Regimes and Educational Development in Cameroon* (Spears Media Press, 2018), 74.

6. Gwanfogbe, *Changing Regimes*, 74.

7. See, for instance, Francisco O. Ramirez and John Boli, "The Political Construction of Mass Schooling: European Origins and Worldwide Institutionalization," *Sociology of Education* 60, no. 1 (1987): 2–17; Daniel Tröhler, Thomas S. Popkewitz, and David F. Labaree, eds., *Schooling and the Making of Citizens in the Long Nineteenth Century: Comparative Visions* (New York: Routledge, 2011).

8. Christian Ydesen, ed., *The OECD's Historical Rise in Education* (Palgrave Macmillan, 2019); Regula Bürgi, "Systemic Management of Schools: The OECD's Professionalisation and Dissemination of Output Governance in the 1960s," *Paedagogica Historica* 52, no. 4 (2016): 408–422.

9. James A. Hazlett, "A History of the National Assessment of Educational Progress, 1963–1973: A Look at Some Conflicting Ideas and Issues in Contemporary American," (PhD diss., University of Kansas, 1974).

10. Daniel Tröhler, "Harmonizing the Educational Globe: World Polity, Cultural Features, and the Challenges to Educational Research," *Studies in Philosophy and Education* 29, no. 1 (2010): 5–17.

11. Joe Heim, "On the World Stage, U.S. Students Fall Behind," *Washington Post,* December 6, 2016, https://www.washingtonpost.com /local/education/on-the-world-stage-us-students-fall-behind/2016/12 /05/610e1e10-b740-11e6-a677-b608fbb3aaf6_story.html; Dana Goldstein, "'It Just Isn't Working': PISA Test Scores Cast Doubt on U.S. Education Efforts," *New York Times,* December 3, 2019, https://www.nytimes.com/2019/12/03/us/us-students-international -test-scores.html; Tawnell D. Hobbs, "U.S. Students Fail to Make Gains Against International Peers," *Wall Street Journal,* December 3, 2019, https://www.wsj.com / articles / u-s-students-fail-to-make-gains -against-international-peers-11575360000.

12. Fernando Reimers, "What Singapore Can Teach the US about Education," *US News and World Report,* July 8, 2016; Anu Partanen, "What Americans Keep Ignoring about Finland's School Success," *The Atlantic,* December 29, 2011.

13. David Labaree, "Let's Measure What No One Teaches: PISA, NCLB, and the Shrinking Aims of Education," *Teachers College Record* 116, no. 9 (2014): 1–14; Heinz-Dieter Meyer and Aaron Benavot, eds., *PISA, Power, and Policy: The Emergence of Global Educational Governance* (Symposium Books Ltd, 2013).

14. Gumm Imsen, Ulf Blossing, and Lejf Moos, "Reshaping the Nordic Education Model in an Era of Efficiency: Changes in the Comprehensive School Project in Denmark, Norway, and Sweden since the Millennium," *Scandinavian Journal of Educational Research* 61, no. 5 (2017): 568–583.

15. Goh Yan Han, "New PSLE Scoring System: MOE Releases Cut-Off Points for Singapore's Secondary Schools," *The Straits Times,* April 27, 2021, https://www.straitstimes.com/singapore/parenting-education /moe-releases-cut-off-points-for-secondary-schools-under-new-psle; Amelia Teng, "PSLE Scoring Revamp: T-Score Replaced by Eight Wider Grade Bands in 2021," *The Straits Times*, July 14, 2016.

Chapter 7. Homegrown Experiments

1. Grant Wiggins, "The Case for Authentic Assessment," *Practical Assessment, Research, and Evaluation* 2, no. 2 (1990), https://doi.org/10.7275 /ffb1-mm19.

2. Wiggins, "The Case for Authentic Assessment."

3. Julie Cohen, Ethan Hutt, Rebekah L. Berlin, Hannah M. Mathews, Jillian P. McGraw, and Jessica Gottlieb, "Sense Making and Professional Identity in the Implementation of edTPA," *Journal of Teacher Education* 71, no. 1 (2020): 9–23.

4. Next Generation Science Standards, "NGSS Leson Screener: A Quick Look at Potential NGSS Lesson Design," https://www.nextgenscience .org/sites/default/files/NGSSScreeningTool-2.pdf.

5. This history is offered in excellent detail in John L. Rudolph, *How We Teach Science: What's Changed, and Why It Matters* (Cambridge, MA: Harvard University Press, 2019).

6. In the context of a seemingly easier problem, assessing and supporting changes in teacher practice required by the shift to the Common Core State Standards, there is a concern that the instruction called for by the

standards and the systems we have in place for assessing instruction under those standards are fundamentally incompatible. Our methods for observing instructional quality in teacher practice (much like our systems for evaluating students) are fundamentally focused on observable elements of classroom practice, while many of the desired goals—collaboration among colleagues across grade levels, the selection of skill appropriate reading materials—are extremely difficult to see or measure through existing evaluation systems, if at all. See Julie Cohen, Ethan Hutt, Rebekah Berlin, and Emily Wiseman, "The Change We Cannot See: Instructional Quality and Classroom Observation in the Era of Common Core," *Educational Policy* (2020), https://doi.org/10.1177/0895904820951114.

7. Brian Stecher, "Local Benefits and Burdens of Large-Scale Portfolio Assessments," *Assessment in Education* 5, no. 3 (1998): 346.

8. Stecher, "Local Benefits and Burdens," 346.

9. Daniel Koretz, "Large-Scale Portfolio Assessments in the US: Evidence Pertaining to the Quality of Measurement," *Assessment in Education* 5, no. 3 (1998): 332. See also Daniel Koretz, Brian Stecher, Stephen Klein, and Daniel McCaffrey, "The Vermont Portfolio Assessment Program: Findings and Implications," *Educational Measurement: Issues and Practice* 13, no. 3 (1994): 5–16.

10. Jay Mathews, "Portfolio Assessment: Carrying Less Weight in the Era of Standards-Based Accountability," *Education Next* 3, no. 3 (2004): 72–76, http://www.educationnext.org/20043/72.html.

11. Quoted in Gail Robinson, "NYC Schools That Skip Standardized Tests Have Higher Graduation Rates," *Hechinger Report,* October 30, 2015, https://hechingerreport.org/nyc-schools-that-skip-standardized-tests-have-higher-graduation-rates/.

12. Starr Sackstein, "Instead of Standardized Testing Consider Portfolio Assessment," *Education Week,* April 29, 2019, https://www.edweek.org/teaching-learning/opinion-instead-of-standardized-testing-consider-portfolio-assessment/2019/04.

13. https://www.evergreen.edu/evaluations.

14. Howard Kirschenbaum, Rodney Napier, and Sidney B. Simon, *Wad-Ja-Get?: The Grading Game in American Education* (New York: Hart Publishing Company, 1971).

15. Tanya Schevitz, "UC Santa Cruz to Start Using Letter Grades," *SF Gate* (Feb. 24, 2000), https://www.sfgate.com/education/article/UC -Santa-Cruz-To-Start-Using-Letter-Grades-2773570.php; Megha Satayanarayana, "UC Santa Cruz Faculty Votes to End Mandatory Student Evaluations," *Santa Cruz Sentinel*, April 24, 2010; Kay Mills, "Changes at 'Oxford on the Pacific': UC Santa Cruz turns to Engineering and Technology," *National Cross Talk,* Spring 2001, http://www.highereducation.org/crosstalk/ct0401/news0401 -changesoxfordpacific.shtml.

16. May L. Smallwood, *An Historical Study of Examinations Grading Systems in Early American Universities* (Cambridge, MA: Harvard University Press, 1935).

17. H. M. Davidovicz, *Pass-Fail Grading—A Review* (Hempstead, NY: Hofstra University Center for the Study of Higher Education, 1972).

18. Arthur Levine and John Weingart, *Reform of Undergraduate Education* (San Francisco: Jossey-Bass, 1973).

19. John E. Bevan, John E. D'Andrea, James Moore, Frances E. Ruller, and Gerald Cate, "Transcript Adequacy—P's, F's and Other Letters," *College and University* 44, no. 4 (1969): 502–503.

20. Bonnie M. Miller, "Can a Pass / Fail Grading System Adequately Reflect Student Progress?" Commentary, *AMA Journal of Ethics* 11, no. 11 (2009): 842–846.

21. Davidovicz, *Pass-Fail Grading—A Review.*

22. David J. Otto, *A Study of the Pass / Fail Grading System.* Office of Institutional Research and Planning, University of Alberta (1972).

23. William Stallings and H. Richard Smock, "The Pass-Fail Grading Option at a State University: A Five Semester Evaluation," *Journal of Educational Measurement* 8, no. 3 (Fall 1971): 153–160.

24. E. Dewey, *The Dalton Laboratory Plan* (New York: E. F. Dutton and Co., 1922).

25. Tammy Bunn Hiller and Amy B. Hietapelto, "Contract Grading: Encouraging Commitment to the Learning Process through Voice in the Evaluation Process," *Journal of Management Education* 25, no. 6 (2001): 660–684.

26. Linda B. Nilson, *Specifications Grading: Restoring Rigor, Motivating Students, and Saving Faculty Time* (Sterling, VA: Stylus Publishing, 2014), xiii.

27. "Micro-Credentials: A Promising Way to Put Educators' Skills Front and Center," Digital Promise, https://digitalpromise.org/2016/02/22/micro-credentials-a-promising-way-to-put-educators-skills-front-and-center/.

28. Brian A. Jacob and Lars Lefgren, "Remedial Education and Student Achievement: A Regression-Discontinuity Analysis," *The Review of Economics and Statistics,* 86, no. 1 (2004): 226–244; Brian A. Jacob and Lars Lefgren, "The Effect of Grade Retention on High School Completion," *American Economic Journal: Applied Economics* 1, no. 3 (2009): 33–58; Guido Schwerdt, Martin R. West, and Marcus A. Winters, "The Effects of Test-Based Retention on Student Outcomes over Time: Regression Discontinuity Evidence from Florida," *Journal of Public Economics* 152 (2017): 154–169; Linda Pagani, Richard E. Tremblay, Frank Vitaro, Bernard Boulerice, and Pierre McDuff, "Effects of Grade Retention on Academic Performance and Behavioral Development," *Development and Psychopathology* 13, no. 2 (2001): 297–315.

Chapter 8. Sustaining Learning

1. See, for instance, Morgan Polikoff, *Beyond Standards: The Fragmentation of Education Governance and the Promise of Curricular Reform* (Cambridge, MA: Harvard Education Press, 2021).

2. For more on this, see Denise Clark Pope, *Doing School: How We Are Creating a Generation of Stressed-Out, Materialistic, and Miseducated Students* (New Haven, CT: Yale University Press, 2008).

3. The major obstacle for states seeking flexibility was the requirement that states achieve a 95 percent student participation rate in annual testing. This requirement prevents states from adopting alternatives such as representative sampling, which is done for examinations like NAEP. Depending on how the sample is constructed (and depending on reporting purposes), representative sampling might produce the added benefit of designing annual assessments that cover a greater portion of the curriculum because each child would not have to take

the entirety of each test. Cedar Attanasio, "Education Officials Seek Flexibility on Student Testing," *Associated Press* (February 26, 2021), https://apnews.com/article/new-mexico-coronavirus-pandemic -student-testing-e13b5a5b498e2164eee003133abd4e76; California Department of Education, "State Board of Education Votes to Seek Federal Assessment Accountability and Reporting Flexibilities Due to Impact of COVID-19 on Schools" (February 24, 2021), https://www .cde.ca.gov/nr/ne/yr21/yr21rel11.asp.

4. Mike Rose, *Possible Lives: The Promise of Public Education in America* (New York: Houghton Mifflin, 1995).

5. Joshua Goodman, Oded Gurantz, and Jonathan Smith, "Take two! SAT Retaking and College Enrollment Gaps," *American Economic Journal: Economic Policy* 12, no. 2 (2020): 115–158.

6. Here we mean validity in the psychometric sense—that it measures what it purports to. For more, see American Educational Research Association, American Psychiatric Association, and National Council on Measurement in Education, "Standards for Educational and Psychological Testing" (Washington, DC: AERA, APA, NCME, 2014), https://www.testingstandards.net/uploads/7/6/6/4/76643089 /standards_2014edition.pdf.

Conclusion

1. Horst W. J. Rittel and Melvin M. Webber, "Dilemmas in a General Theory of Planning," *Policy Sciences* 4, no. 2 (1973): 155–169.

2. We are grateful to our mentor Larry Cuban for his distinction between problems and dilemmas.

Acknowledgments

For the past fifteen years, we've been privileged to have each other as friends and collaborators. This book was the product of our shared interests, and it emerged from conversations that began when we were graduate students together, sharing a (fairly wretched) basement office.

Yet books don't emerge from camaraderie alone. Instead, they emerge from ideas. And ideas, in turn, emerge from communities. Inasmuch as that is the case, there are several communities that we wish to acknowledge for the role they played in the creation of this book.

The first of those communities is the group of mentors who shaped so much of our thinking about schools, history, and the purpose of scholarship. David Labaree, Larry Cuban, and the late, great David Tyack taught us to always begin our explanations about the present by starting with a look at the past. How did we get here? Where have we been? What can we learn from those who preceded us? These kinds of questions, and the impulse to ask them, are our inheritance from these scholars. We are grateful to them for the investments of time and support they made in us long ago. Their generosity of spirit and the engaged scholarship they modeled continue to guide us in our careers.

The second community we need to thank is the largely amorphous group of colleagues who have been our companions in thought over the past decade and a half. We like to think that the ideas in this book belong to us. But of course they don't. Without the push and pull of other scholars, our ideas would be ours alone, but they wouldn't be worth publishing. We're grateful to our colleagues at the University of Massachusetts Lowell and the University of North Carolina at Chapel Hill, to our peers in educational research, to our collaborators at other research universities, and to all of those who collectively shape the ecosystem of ideas in which we are fortunate enough to work.

We also want to acknowledge the important role played by the very first intellectual communities that we joined. From an early age, each of us was cared for by our teachers, who taught us the kinds of inspiring places schools could be. And from an even earlier age, each of us was cared for by our families—in Ethan's case, a family that included siblings Marcie, Amanda, and Denver—who opened up the world of ideas for us. We are particularly grateful to our parents, who taught us much of what we know and most of who we are.

Finally, we want to acknowledge our partners, Katie Henderson and Daniel Klasik, as well as, in Jack's case, his daughter Annabelle. Our ideas, after all, don't emerge from some part of us that lives only in the office or the library. They emerge from our whole selves. Each of us is lucky to be loved.

Index